TRADITIONS AND RITUALS

Incredible India

TRADITIONS & RITUALS

Muthusamy Varadarajan

wisdom
tree
ACADEMIC

By arrangement with
Department of Tourism, Ministry of Culture, Government of India

To my own trinity — Krishna, Kabir & Satya

Published in 2007 by

wisdom tree

Wisdom Tree
4779/23 Ansari Road, Darya Ganj, New Delhi-110002
Ph: 23247966/67/68

Text © Muthusamy Varadarajan

Photographs
Prem Kapoor - 11,61,65,66,72,77; Parmarth Niketan - 13,33,35,38,43,51;
Author - 12,15,19,22,23,41,52,60,83,91,96,97,99,101
Phal Girota - 18,69; Isha Foundation - 47,55
Incredible India - 57,92,100,103; Fawzan Hussain - 84;
National Museum - 2; Siddharth - 4

ISBN   81-8328-066-8

Conceptualised and published by Shobit Arya for Wisdom Tree; *edited by* Manju Gupta; *designed
at* SN Graphix *and printed at* Print Perfect, New Delhi - 110064

Preface

The writing of this book took me on a voyage back into my childhood and adolescence and handed me back to the era of advancing age. In the process, as I delved into events and incidents, revisited temples (*kshetratana*) and rivers and seas (*teertha yatra*), and festivals and celebrations, the flashback that memory vouchsafed to me aided and enthralled me.

Rituals had been an integral part of my life, from the time my father, often away on tour or engrossed in his duties as a policeman, after a day-long fast each month on the day of *Kritigai* in honour of Kartikeya, could not himself do the *puja* to the Lord, without which he could not break his fast. On the *pandit's* assurance that his son could officiate at this fascinating task, I was oftentimes commissioned, right from the time I was about seven, to do the *puja*. And, as I grew up, and my father was no more, my mother would have me perform the annual Rama Navami *puja* for Rama, her *ishta devata*.

And, of course, during the best part of my young life, travelling with my parents all over India, I had the opportunity to visit temples and to bathe in holy waters, go round sacred hills (*giri pradakshina*), have a glimpse of the Chidambara *rahasyam* at the Golden Hall of Nataraja, or witness the Kartigai lamp being lit at the peak of the Arunachala hill, after a *darshan* of Bhagwan Sri Ramana. I have traversed many a village around Tiruchi and Thanjavur (in Tamil Nadu) with my *sanyasin* grandfather Gnananandendra Saraswati, as he stood before homes, intoning *Bhavati bhiksham dehi*, and received alms. All these, coupled with the fact that my grandparents and uncles and aunts galore from both sides of the family sang *stotras* every morning in the most dulcet and appealing of *ragas*, my mother did Deepalakshmi *puja* every Friday for five decades and did *asvatta pradakshina* on *Somavara amavasya*, and my father sang lovely hymns in our mother tongue to his favourite deity Muruga (as the Tamils call Kartikeya), ignited a small spark in me very early on in life. The spark has endured.

Traditions handed down generations were explained to me; more importantly, they were observed by my parents and demonstrated to me in practice, by one or the other member of my vast joint family — traditions that were not of the Tamil or the Indian, but verily traditions of the salt of the earth the world over.

The best part of all this was that, invariably, my parents and elders explained to me the why and where for of each ritual or tradition. This is what led me to happily embark on this book. Half a century ago, when I sat for the competitive examination for the Civil Services, I had to write an essay on 'If Youth Knew, if Age Could'. It is the same story here — thoughtless disbelief would give way to understanding if only the elders could supply the *raison*

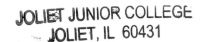

d'etre of things. And even if many rituals are, or can no longer be, observed as in days of yore, one would at least know why our ancients did. If this feeble effort of mine contributes to the dawn of that understanding, I would be more than happy. Far be it from me to mandate the performance of any ritual, or every ritual; but I would certainly say, "Perform or not any ritual, as you wish, but understand its significance and do it or ignore it!"

My deep debt of gratitude goes to Alka Sinha who spent days and weeks researching for the material; to my learned friend Professor A. Sampathnarayan, formerly of Rashtriya Sanskrit Sansthan, for his monumental labour in going through my manuscript and assisting me with his incisive analysis and suggestions; to Dr Varsha Das, the editor, for her patience; to my caring and wise friends Updesh Kaur Bevil and Santhanam Iyer who gave me valuable insights on rites and relevant texts of Sikh and Hindu lore respectively; to my son Tunku Varadarajan who, with his wife Amy, took time off his busy days and nights with the *Wall Street Journal,* New York to edit the final version that emerged from my computer; to Shashi Banerjee who patiently helped me go through the first edited version as well as refine and compact it; to my publisher Shobit Arya who was often exasperated but always cloaked it with an indulgent smile; to my children Rathi, Sunit, Nandini and Siddharth and to many friends whose patience equalled their trust in me.

I dedicate the book to my parents Lakshmi and Ombalapady Appasamy Muthusamy, without whose care, concern and personal example, my education, formal and non-formal, would have remained incomplete.

Muthusamy Varadarajan

Contents

Editor's Note

India, home to one of the most ancient civilisations, is a unique example of cultural and geographical diversities. Dissimilar cultural practices are deeply rooted in people's daily lives even in the 21st century. Indian history is the fruit of geography, and geography the root of history. The history of several millennia has merged with phenomenal geographical variations to create the incredible India of today.

India is incredible in its landscapes, and the people who adorn her. Its rituals and traditions; sculptures and paintings; dance, music and theatre; handicrafts, fairs and festivals; monuments and manuscripts; and its varied cuisine — each is a definite statement that only India can proudly pronounce.

Myriad streams and rivers have been flowing for centuries in their own special terrain, sometimes forceful, sometimes gentle. Despite all kinds of obstacles, they flow on. When these waters reach the ocean, they mingle, and become one huge ocean. Similarly, these diverse, astonishingly rich and colourful cultural currents create a harmonious hymn known as India, even as they retain their unique individual identity.

This series of Incredible India presents 10 books on different cultural aspects of the country, written by well-known experts on the subject. Muthusamy Varadarajan, the author, is fortunate enough to witness most of the rituals and traditions described in this book.

Traditions are not mere dogmatic beliefs. They include religious rites, habitual actions and customs of a community or a group of people who live together at the same place. Religion in its pure form is highly individualistic but when it is performed as a ritual, the whole community participates in it. In the magico-religious ceremonies of the Vedic Aryans, rituals were combined with myths. They continue to be the same in the 21st century. However, a modern Indian is free to exercise his/her freedom of choice. As a result one finds variations in rituals from place to place, and from person to person. It is no longer a rural-urban divide. It is either a choice or societal pressure. But they survive indeed!

The author has covered a large number of rituals and traditions in the context of the life cycle. This cycle begins when the life is still in the mother's womb. Innumerable ceremonies are performed throughout the journey from womb to tomb. He has extensively quoted from Sanskrit and Tamil literature, both of which are ancient; the latter being his mother tongue. Due to cultural diversities some stages of life have interestingly different rituals and beliefs. Indians in general love to celebrate, at times even death.

1 | Samskaras — Then and Now

Myths and rituals are as old as humankind. Bewilderment at Nature's vagaries, fear of the unknown and inability to reason either of them out led to their genesis and to the belief in one and observance of the other. Peals of thunder, flashes of lightning, tempests and storms, scorching heat, freezing cold, deluges, parched earth — all these terrified man. But when things became milder, he saw the blue cloud yielding benevolent and seasonal rain, the arid earth lapping up water from the skies, and plants started growing, turned green and yielded grain and fruit. And he saw that the gentle breeze cooled him, wafted his tiny craft over the waters of the rivers and the seas, guiding him to shoals of fish and piloted him back to havens of comfort and safety on land. Thus perhaps, it was that he came to believe that powerful and unseen forces had to be propitiated in some way or the other to make them friendly. A system of myths and a regimen of rituals thus emerged.

Rituals started to govern the conduct of man in his daily life through traditional usage and precedent; in course of time, handed down in writing too, except in cases where the rituals had acquired mere social content but not religious prescription. Significantly, religion entered into the picture at some point, with the result that most of the religions of the world even today have a set of rituals concerning birth, marriage, conduct of life and death.

Hindu rituals are termed *samskaras,* basically meaning rites that 'purify' one at each stage of life. Starting from the merely superstitious and propitiatory, a cultural and moral purpose gradually informed the *samskaras,* as the role and significance of the community gained in strength. Rituals not only purified man at various stages of his life, but also emerged as tools of expression, of joy, sense of achievement, sorrow as well as the channels through which material rewards could be solicited and obtained, like *mrityunjaya homam* for longevity and *putrakameshti yajna* for progeny.

Precise social purpose was also built into the *samskaras* — like the *upanayan*a, investiture of the sacred thread, leading to the guru and signifying the formal commencement of one's education and the *samavartana,* conclusion, or the *vivaha,* wedding ceremony, signalling that one has embarked on a new phase of life as *grihasta,* householder. Last but not least, the punctilious performance of the *samskaras* also vouchsafes *moksha,* salvation, unto him that has performed them with *shraddha,* sincerity — *Brahmanah padam avapnoti yasmat na chyavate punah,* verily he attains Brahmanhood from where he will never be displaced.

The substantive purpose too was that, properly understood and sincerely performed, the *samskaras* helped foster the formation of character and

personality. This is corroborated by Dr Rajbali Pandey*: "The *samskaras* were never regarded as ends in themselves. They were expected to grow and ripen into moral virtues…the ethical attempt for the moral uplift of an individual is (also) visible." While he concludes, "This stage of the *samskaras* marks a great advance over the individual benefits that were solicited in them", it was also "the business of the *samskaras* to make the body a valuable possession, a thing not to be discarded, but made holy; a thing to be sanctified, so that it might be a fitting instrument of the spiritual intelligence embodied in it."

The *samskaras* were thus a happy blend of the individual's development and well-being, taking into context the social and cultural milieu and a means of realising the symbiotic relationship between an active life and spiritual aspirations, they aided in letting one lead a life of *dharma,* right conduct. Unfortunately, intervening eras of extreme rigidity ensued, when change

ABOVE
A homa in progress: ghee *(clarified butter) being offered* as ahuti

* Dr Rajbali Pandey: *Hindu Samskaras — Socio-religious Study of the Hindu Sacraments*, Motilal Banarsidass, 1949

from what was prescribed was absolutely taboo, when no heed was paid to changed and changing needs or to the conditions of life and society and when *mantras* or chants sanctified by the inexorable passage of time, which protect the reciter thereof — *Mantaaram traayate iti mantraha* — were chanted in a language that had ceased to be the current vehicle of interpersonal communication. With the joint family system disintegrating, and the inevitable pressures of daily life in the modern age, the real import of the rituals has almost totally ceased to be understood.

What needs to be appreciated is that *samskaras* in the Hindu tradition are an ingredient of the *karma marga,* path of action, the other two being the *upaasana marga,* path of worship and meditation, and *jnana marga,* path of knowledge. *Samskaras* are the first step in the ladder of preparedness for the other two stages that culminate in *chitta shuddhi,* purification of the mind-consciousness.

LEFT
A young brahmachari *in* sukhasana, *doing the* Gayatri japa

ABOVE
Tradition and modernity: brahmacharis *at the computer*

2 | Vivaha — What God Hath Joined

The caveman might have started off wielding the club against his woman, but soon realised that he could not do without her either. One does not know at what point the idea of marriage and family took shape, but soon it became the cornerstone of life in all climes, continents and races. For, it imparted unassailable stability (at least in ages gone by) and solidity to human existence by catering to the entire spectrum of physical, emotional, psychological and spiritual needs.

The institution of marriage was a veritable anchor of the ship of life, at least till lately — with the concept of 'till death doth us part' — be it in the Christian sacrament or the Hindu *samskara*. Even in a religion prescribing contractual marriage, the concept of a casual 'at man's will' divorce has come increasingly under fire, both from religious reformists women's groups. The idea is that, be it sanctioned by contract or sanctified by custom and ceremony, 'marriage' calls for (and generally receives) respect and cannot be dissolved merely at one's whim.

Perhaps in no other religion is it more so than in Hinduism. Although the *ashrama*, stage of life of a *grihasta*, householder, ranks second in an array of four, and the *vivaha* ceremony is the thirteenth in a series of *shodasa*, 16 rituals in a Hindu's life, it has been chosen to lead off this work as it is the starting point of a union of Shiva and Shakti, the male and female principles, aimed at the creation of progeny. All other incidents of life, from conception to death, are concomitant to this union, the householder being the fulcrum.

In ancient India, as many as eight different forms of *vivaha*, were in vogue — like *paisaacha*, obtaining the bride through pretence and artifice, *raakshasa*, taking a wife by force, *gandharva*, by mutual choice of man and woman, *asura*, by paying the bride-price and *brahma*, giving away of the bride by the father, with the conferment of gifts and ornaments on a man of character. The present-day 'love marriages' may in a loose way be said to correspond to the *gandharva* form! The stipulation and extraction of dowry or bride price does not seem to have been an accepted element of marriage in ancient times, although we do come across *stridhana*, a father's gifts to the bride at her marriage, but this was obviously voluntary.

ABOVE
Flowers, fruits, betel leaves and the mangalasutra *at a ceremonial display on an auspicious red* sari *at a* vivaha *in south India*

ABOVE
Panigrahanam,
where the groom takes
the bride's right palm
in his own; the hands
of the bride are
hennaed in gorgeous
designs

Due heed was paid to the lineage of the families on both sides (redolent of anxious Victorian matrons keeping an eagle's eye on 'eligible' suitors from reputed, and of course, wealthy families for their debutante daughters!), with particular reference to the bar on exogamy through avoidance of *sagotra*, belonging to the same *gotra*, lineage.

Apart from the *sagotra* taboo, there were other *laukika*, material or practical, considerations for selecting the bride — principally wealth, beauty, intellect and of course, family. There were very rigorous and specific prescriptions on what kind of physical characteristics and mental make-up rendered a prospective bride undesirable. The bridegroom was no less rigorously assessed. One such is laid down in the *Samskara Prakasa* to the effect that the groom must be a man of learning, that is, he must be a *brahmachari*, one who has successfully completed his education, possesses good character, has affable friends of equally esteemed character and is endowed with becoming modesty and humility. As in the case of the bride, specific 'for' and 'against' physical traits and moral characteristics were also prescribed for the groom.

All prescriptions as to family, beauty, intellect and character being thus confirmed, the *vivaha* follows. The ceremony is scheduled for an auspicious *muhurtam*, the day and time identified after a careful examination of the stars and the seasons. Normally it is when the sun is in the northern hemisphere, in the days of the waxing moon and during a precise time-span arrived at on astrological considerations and computations. Some months of the year are totally taboo for *vivaha*.

As many as 40 steps in the *vivaha* rituals are on record. Obviously, with couples who are in a perpetual hurry today, with guests and relatives being in even greater hurry, the emphasis is on brevity. The Arya Samaj *vivaha* format caters to this, without sacrificing the essence.

Essentially the rituals include *vaagdaanam*, betrothal, where a public exchange of the undertaking to give away the bride and an avowal of the same by the groom and family take place. This was a special ceremony in the olden days, often much before the actual date of marriage. Now it is conducted as *nischayataartham*, in the south or *sagaai* in the north.

After the pre-nuptial bath by the bride and the groom, the groom proceeds to the bride's place in a procession of relatives and friends to the accompanying strains of *mangala vadyas,* auspicious musical wind instruments, like the *shehnai* and the *nadaswaram.* In the south, the procession is usually on foot or in a highly bedecked car or carriage; in the north, the groom is often seated on a horse and is piloted by the *baraat,* the groom's family and friends. On arrival, the groom is welcomed by the womenfolk of the bride's family, with music and song and offerings of flowers and lamps.

Madhuparkam is the honour proffered to the groom at that point by the bride's father — through *paadyam*, offering of water for washing hands and feet, and *arghyam,* offering water to sip; milk and honey are also offered. The

groom sprinkles a few drops of water on and touches various parts of his body, invoking speech and sight, energy and strength.

The bride arrives and is seated with the groom before the sacred fire, usually produced by friction between a few wood pieces from the *peepul* or *udambara* tree. She then receives her nuptial garment and wears it. The couple is anointed (*samanjana*) by the bride's father, while the groom invokes the gods to unite the hearts that come together on the auspicious occasion.

The ceremony commences with a brief *puja*, defined as 'the ceremonial act of showing reverence to a god or goddess through invocation, prayer, song and ritual' (Stephen P. Huyler).* The *puja* is to Vighneswara, the elephant-headed Divine remover of obstructions and obstacles, followed by choral chanting of select portions of *sukhtam* (derived from the *Upanishads* that date back to 800-400 BC), like *Sree Sukhtam* to celebrate the bounty of the earth and cattle, and *Purusha Sukhtam*, to hail the creation of the universe and the variegated life forms that abound in it, and salute the forces that sustain them, as also to pray for the welfare of the couple and for healthy and noble progeny.

The important step of *kanya daanam*, gifting of the virgin bride, ensues. In the absence of the father of the bride, the grandfather, the brother, elders of the same *gotra*, caste, or also the mother (early feminism) are entitled to do it. This process

*Stephen P. Huyler: *Meeting God — Elements of Hindu Devotion*, Yale University Press, 1999

is accompanied by an incantation avowing that it was being done to ensure the happiness of 12 preceding and 12 succeeding generations through the progeny resulting from the union.

The father exhorts the groom that in the pursuit of *dharma, artha* and *kama*, piety, wealth and desire, she is not to be violated. *Naaticharaami*, I will not, assures the groom.

The groom asks then: "Who has gifted her to me?"

The answer is *Kama,* Deity of Love, signifying that their conjoint lives may never run dry of love. It is significant here to recall that Shri Krishna himself has said in the *Bhagavad Gita:* "I am desire (love) that does not run counter to *dharma.*" Thus one may say that in the context of *vivaha* too, love is sacred and supreme, yoking as it does two beings together for life.

Traditions & Rituals   19

Next comes the *mangalya dhaaranam*, the investiture of the *mangalasutra*, chord of auspiciousness, which is in the form of a turmeric-soaked thread. Taking it in his hands, the groom recites:

Maangalyam tantuna anena mama jeevana hetunaa
kante badhnaami subhage tvam jeevam saradah shatam.

This is a sacred thread. Oh bride of many auspicious traits, may you live happily for a hundred years with me!

ABOVE
The groom ties the mangalasutra *around the bride's neck*

RIGHT
Saptapadi, *the seven steps of the Hindu couple going round the sacred fire, constituting irrevocable proof of the* vivaha

With these words, the groom ties the *mangalasutra* in a knot around the bride's neck, and then (usually in the south) the groom's sister standing behind the bride ties two more knots. It is followed these days by a golden rope chain, with two small golden discs in front etched with *tulsi*, basil plant, the favourite of Vishnu, again affirming love and lasting togetherness. Of course, custom varies in this behalf: in Maharashtra, for instance, instead of the gold chain, a collection of exquisite black beads strung in gold forms the *mangalasutra*. In the south, the tying of this secular symbol is greeted with the ecstatic and high-pitched music of the *tavil*, percussion, and the *nadaswaram*. In Bengal and Orissa, jubilant ululation, which is redolent of the custom from the Middle East too, marks the occasion. Interestingly, *ululukaranam*, ululation, is prescribed in the *Grihya Sutras*. It is customary for the *pandits*, priests and elders to bless the bride with the words, *Sumangaleeriyam vadhuh imam samedha pashyata saubhagyam asmai dattva yaataasthyam viparetana*, may this confer all prosperity on thy husband as also help you to lead a conforming life. Turmeric-mixed rice and flowers are showered on the couple in a time-honoured gesture of benediction.

This is followed by offering *homams*, oblations, to *Agni*, God of Fire, the chief of which is the *laajahoma*, invoking opulence and progeny. The bride's younger brother pours parched rice into her hands who, joining hands with her husband, offers it unto the fire, praying for long life and welfare.

This is the moment of the *panigrahanam*, where the groom takes the hand of the bride in his hands. In *Valmiki Ramayanam*, as King Janaka gifts his daughter Sita to Rama, in the verse commencing thus: *Iyam Sita mama suta*, he exhorts Rama:

"Here is my daughter who henceforth shall be your partner in all your prescribed *dharma*. Take her right hand in your right hand and be blessed. She will be faithful unto you, bring you the best of luck and will follow you like a shadow forever." Equal partnership in the pursuit of *dharma* is what stands out here.

It is the beginning of a new and purposeful relationship. As he clasps his wife's hands, the groom intones: *Grahnaami te suprajaastvaaya hastam,* my bride, I hold your name with the prayer that, living with me, you will give birth to noble children. The gods, Bhaga, Aryama, Surya and Indra have given you unto me so that I may perform the duties of a householder.

This is followed by the ritual called *asma arohana*, when the bride steps on a stone to the recitation of "Tread on this stone, be firm and immovable (unchanging) like it." This signifies her commitment to lifelong faithfulness to the marriage vows. The bride is also asked to look heavenward and espy the *Dhruva Nakshatra*, the Pole Star, undeterred from its path — the child-devotee Dhruva of the *Puranas* and whose commitment to Vishnu was unswerving despite 100 terrors visited upon him at the instance of his stepmother. The bride is also asked to espy Arundhati, Sage Vashishta's wife whose chastity was matchless, as also the *saptarishi mandala*, the constellation of seven sages.

What follows is the *saptapadi*, the seven steps, northward around the sacred fire, next to the *mangalya dhaaranam*, the most significant element of the *vivaha* ritual. Walking hand in hand, with a corner of the groom's *angavastram*, upper cloth, tied to one end of the bride's sari, the former invokes various deities. The first step is to the intoning of *Ekam ishe Vishnu tvaanvedu,* may Vishnu follow thee, then *dhwe urje,* for strength, *trinee vrataaya,* for observance of religious vows, *chatwari mayobhavaaya,* for happiness, *pancha pashubhya,* for the welfare

of cattle, *shat ritubhya,* for good and orderly seasons, and the seventh, *sapta saptabhyo hotraapyo Vishnus tvaanvetu,* may Vishnu follow thee for the performance of religious practices in full measure and substance!

Reaffirming at this point the fullness and inviolateness of their union, the groom not only tells the wife, "May you with the seventh step be united to and devoted unto me for life!" but reassures her, "This I am; that art thou. The *saman,* musical rendering of the *Rk,* I, the *Rk,* one-quarter of a verse which is complete, with meaning, thou. The Heaven I, the Earth thou…Let us unite, let us beget progeny. Loving, resplendent with burgeoning minds, let us see, live and hear a hundred autumns!"

Saptapadi is the one irrefutable proof that the wedding has been solemnised. This is also recognised in Indian civil law.

PAGE 22
Asma arohana,
where the Hindu
bride steps on a stone,
signifying rocklike
stability in marriage

PAGE 23
Sindhura daanam,
the Bengali groom
applying sindhura
(vermillion) on the
bride's hair parting;
he is to look away as
he does it (top); the
same ritual in north
India (bottom)

RIGHT
Bidai, tearful
farewell, as the bride
leaves her parents'
home for her
husband's, after the
wedding

The bridegroom touches the heart of the bride, invoking Lord Prajapati to join heart to heart, mind to mind and will to will — emphasising that healthy and happy emotions and feelings are and shall forever be at the core of the union. Then comes the *sindhura daanam,* when the groom applies *sindhura,* vermillion, in the parting of the hair on the bride's forehead, thus making her a *sumangali,* the auspicious one. This *sindhura (kumkumam* in the south) along with the colourful bangles and bracelets she disports are the eternal marks of a married woman — now a fashion statement and beauty symbol the world over!

A very interesting adjunct of the marriage rites is the *triratra vrata,* continence for three nights. Not eating salty food for three nights and sleeping not in luxury but on the floor, the couple is to refrain from conjugal union for a year, failing which it is for 12 days, or six nights, or in the last analysis, at least for three nights. The *raison d'être* is evidently that this would instil in the young hopefuls the idea that physical passion is not everything, and that love is not a passing emotion or a fleeting frenzy that consumes but does not last, but is indeed one that has to be enjoyed unhurriedly and savoured for long.

The festivities over, the couple departs for the husband's home. This is also the most poignant moment for the bride's father, without doubt in any culture, anywhere in the world. No account can equal that of Kalidasa's description in *Abhijnana Shakuntalam* of how Sage Kanva felt at the departure of his daughter Shakuntala as a result of her *gandharva vivaha* to Dushyanta.

Kanva says: "At the thought that Shakuntala leaves me today, my heart is soaked in grief, my throat is choked, my eyes are moist. My mind stands still. If this should perturb me so, a hermit in the forest, how much more would a mere householder be affected!"

In the north, the moment of the *bidai*, bidding farewell to the bride, when the *doli*, a palanquin, in the old days but nowadays usually a car, leaves the parental home is fraught with intense grief and irrepressible sobs!

The entry of the couple into the husband's home is a happy ritual called *griha pravesam*, entering their new home.

Essentially, the *vivaha* ceremony is a sacrament and bespeaks of myths and is replete with symbols, signalling the abandonment of one's status as bachelor and as virgin. It announces the commencement of a conjoint life, whose goal is the achievement of the four *purusharthas*, things desired by human beings: *dharma*, wide-ranging codes of conduct, *artha*, wealth, *kama*, desires and *moksha*, beatitude, with the last-named to be attained in the fullness of life. Linked are the desire for and the imperative of creating suitable progeny who would carry on the lineage.

3 | The Moment of Birth, the Years of Growth

Marriage follows *upanayana*. What precedes *upanayana*? It is a series of rites of childhood and most of which are performed even today in various parts of the country. Some are no longer practiced as prescribed, including *garbaadhaana*, fertilisation and conception.

Garbaadhaana is, in fact, a prenatal ritual — a sequence of actions that included taking care of prohibited months and the best nights (after the menstrual cycle ended) for conception, and the gender and nature of the offspring (e.g. even night — boy; odd night — girl; ninth night — girl with an auspicious future; tenth night — a wise son, and so on). Based on the premise that marriage imposed on the individual the sacred duty of begetting a son (who would help discharge the debt to ancestors), men approached the wives with this definite purpose (of procreating children) in a definite manner with, in the words of Dr Rajbali Pandey, "the religious serenity which they believed would consecrate the would-be child."

The first ceremony after conception is the *pumsavana,* originally conceived of as the rite that produces a *pumaan,* male child. With the passage of time, currently, it is for the first-born, be it male or female, and for the first-born only. Usually it is celebrated sometime between the third and seventh months. In Tamil Nadu, south India, there is a social event called *valai kaappu,* the protection conferred by bangles, in which there is practically no religious ceremony but just a happy celebration at the home of the woman's mother, mostly by women who foregather around the expectant mother and load her arms with multicoloured bangles of a dazzling variety.

Nowadays, the *pumsavana* is celebrated along with *seemantonnayana.* It is generally in the fifth month after conception, since it is believed: *Panchame manah pratibuddhataram bhavati,* the mind starts forming around the fifth month. From that point onwards, the foetus needs utmost care and scrupulous avoidance of all manners of shock, so that its growth and development are not hampered. The mental and physical well-being of the mother, too, being a matter of great concern, these ceremonies help cheer her and keep her in good and affable humour.

Apart from social and religious ceremonies, there were a number of do's and don'ts for the mother-to-be. Taboos were against bathing in a river, going to a deserted house, subjecting herself to any kind of mental disturbance, family quarrels (that would upset her equanimity), mutilation, hair in disarray, speaking *ashubha,* inauspicious or ill-omened words, eating at dusk, strenuous exercise including swift walking, riding a bullock-cart, a handy vehicle even today in our rural areas, climbing multi-storeyed and tall buildings, mounting an elephant or a horse, consumption of spicy, stale and

RIGHT
Saraswati, Goddess of Learning, deemed to be patron deity who ensures the healthy growth of the foetus

heavy foods and insomnia. Highly recommended, on the other hand, was for her to busy herself with good deeds like giving alms, bathing in herbs-infused warm water, offering worship, deference to elders, and listening to auspicious sounds and music. The sound of the *veena,* a traditional string instrument, regarded as the favourite of Saraswati, the Goddess of Learning, was thought to be especially good for the salubrious development of the foetus and for the quickening of its sensibilities.

The father-to-be was expected to take special care of his wife and meet her wishes always keeping her happy and content. There were prohibitions for him, too, such as not cropping his hair, joining a funeral procession, going on *teertha yatra,* pilgrimage, taking *sindhu snaanam,* a bath in the sea, and indulging in *maithunam,* sexual congress. Some of these might seem incongruous or unreasoned, but most of them were based on very sound principles and mature and scientific understanding of physiology, anatomy and the influence of mind upon matter.

With the usual ceremonial preludes of (the woman) fasting, bathing and wearing new clothes, the preliminary rites were performed, with the obligatory invocations to beneficent deities, dropping into her nostril a few drops

of the juice of banyan *(Ficus indica)* buds, mixed with milk and honey and the juices of assorted herbs like *kusakantaka, somalata, sulakshmana batasunga, sahadevi* and *visvadeva*. She was expected not to let the juice flow out. This was in consonance with a fairly popular medical practice of the ancient times, based on the belief that the juice, particularly of the banyan, had great therapeutic value. It was held to be a surefire preventive against abortion, as well as protective of the expectant mother against other ailments to which she could be prone. As said earlier, the expectation, or the desire in ancient times for a male child was also a result hoped for from such ingestion. This is supported by the fact that a vessel containing water was ceremonially placed on the woman's lap and the husband touched her stomach (womb) while reciting a verse containing the word *suparnosi, parna* meaning 'wing'. The wish thus expressed was that the child should be a handsome little fellow. The pot of water reflected the ancients' obsession with water, signifying the origin, growth and plenitude of life — water having been one of the *pancha bhootas,* the five primordial elements.

But the most significant part of the ceremony is *seemantonnayana,* the parting of the hair of the woman by the husband. She is seated to the west of the sacrificial fire and the husband traces the central parting of her hair, going backwards from the top of the forehead with a collection of some *udumbara* fruits, *darbha,* sacred *kusa* grass, and a 'porcupine quill with three white spots', to the accompaniment of each of the three *mahaa,* supreme, *vyaahritis* — *bhur, bhuvah* and *suvah.*

The husband also usually marks the parting with vermillion — red powder to scare away evil spirits from harming his wife and the child-to-be. He also puts a wreath of the *udumbara* branch or stalk of barley around her neck, auguring fertility and sound progeny. The ceremony concludes with women singing in happy anticipation of heroic offspring; after this, the woman maintains silence till the night when she resumes speech, uttering the aforesaid three *vyaahritis* herself.

Jaatakarma, the actual birth ceremonies, no longer observed in the manner prescribed revolved round the *sutika bhavana* in the home itself, corresponding to the delivery room in a modern hospital. The expectant mother was relegated to this room, which had been carefully (giving regard to the direction) chosen, cleansed and prepared. Fire, water, a lamp, mustard seeds and grains of rice were kept there.

Jaatakarma took place before the umbilical chord was cut. On the announcement of the birth, the father went in and gazed at the infant's face. After a purificatory bath — the delivery room being deemed to be impure for 10 days, at which point *punyahavachanam* was performed — he commenced the ritual by giving the infant a lick of honey and *ghee,* clarified butter, to the accompaniment of the *mahaa vyahritis,* praying to the gods, to herald the dawn of intelligence in the newborn. Apart from being an antidote to many illnesses, *ghee* and honey were seen as the enhancers of memory, intellectual prowess, lustre and health.

On conclusion of this ceremony of *medha janana,* dawn of the intellect, the father along with the *pandits* present, invoked the blessings of assorted Divines like Soma, Agni and Brahman itself, as well as the sacred rivers, the ocean and the *rishis,* sages. All of these being long-lived, these supplications to them ensured a long life for the infant: *Jeevema sharadasshatam,* may you live to see a hundred autumns! It was a prayer and a benediction. Then the navel chord was cut and the baby handed back to the mother for its first taste of its mother's milk.

The ceremonies that followed, like *naamakarana,* christening, *anna praasana,* the first feed with something other than mother's milk — literally, the introduction of *anna,* cooked grain, *chudakarana,* tonsuring, *and karnavedha,* piercing of the earlobe, are invariably performed even today, largely because of the *laukika* aspects. *Nishkramana,* the first outing, is almost never performed while *vidyaarambha,* the ceremonial commencement of education, is not universally celebrated either.

The *naamakarana* is what confers identity on the infant, usually after the perceived impurity resulting from the process of birth is over. Holding the infant on his lap, the father invokes the Divines as was customary and touched the breath of the child. Then he addressed it, by calling out its name into its right ear. The family deity, the month of birth, and the *nakshatra,* star under which it was born, were intoned and with each, the baby was told his/her name.

In olden days, there were numerous criteria for selection of the name — the number of syllables (even for boys and odd for girls), the permissible ending for boys and girls, the traits it should signify (wisdom and sagacity for the Brahmins, valour for the Kshatriyas and economic and business acumen for the Vaishyas), and the stars under which they were born. Interestingly, in the days of Manu, it was laid down that girls should not be named after trees, rivers, hills or constellations. These days, happily, no such taboos are there. Names like Parijatha, Mallika, Ganga, Narmada, Girija, Parvatham, Rohini and Kritika abound.

From birth to the naming ceremony to *karnaveda,* the piercing of the earlobe, as in the case of *chudakarana,* there was the belief that piercing the earlobes of a boy or a girl ensured protection from certain afflictions. Slated usually around the sixteenth day after birth, this ceremony is done in the presence of a close circle of family and friends. The child is seated on the father's lap facing east and with suitable invocations, such as "May good and auspicious things flow through to the ears", the right ear is pierced first and then the left, traditionally by a goldsmith. Depending on the circumstances of the family, a slender gold or silver ring is put through the hole, graduating in later years into a diamond or ruby stud. In fact, pandits well-versed in *Veda paarayana,* recitation of the *Vedas,* display the diamond studs on their ears with aplomb.

The *anna praasana* is the next important ceremony, in the sense that it is in the interest of the mother and the child. Continued breastfeeding would

RIGHT
A child after chudakarana (mundan), *with tonsured head*

affect the health of the former; while it is equally important that the infant, having acquired a set of immunities via mother's milk, is introduced to other forms of food. The basic thrust, thus, is on weaning of the infant at the appropriate time, in the interests of both the mother and child. Usually it was in the sixth month after birth or, in another view, whenever the child was ready to ingest solid foods. While in very ancient days, the feeding consisted even of meat, especially those of certain birds, the current practice is to start off with a puree of rice and milk, graduating to mashed lentils and vegetables, and yoghurt and rice. The rice for the *anna praasana* is cooked with special care and, as usual, with the appropriate pleas to Divine presences soliciting strength, intellect and purity. The father also offers other oblations so that, apart from the palate being pleased and the stomach appeased, the ear, eyes and other senses are also satisfied. The idea is that nourishment ought to cater to all the requirements of mind and body.

Chudakarana (mundan), tonsure, has perhaps a medical basis too. Charaka and Susruta, the legendary practitioners of ancient Indian medicine, prescribed it as a means of removing impurities and imparting delight, affluence, valour, lissomeness and beauty. Very often, and this is observed even now, the first lock of hair that is removed is offered to the *kula devata,* family deity; indeed it is in the almost universal custom to have this done at the premises of that deity's temple.

A large part of this interesting ceremony is centred around the safe and harmless use of the razor over the child's tender head that is shaved. The father being the principal *karta,* performer, he is naturally deemed capable of holding with firmness the squirming baby as the barber wields his razor. The father helps moisten the head, prays to the Divines that there may be no injury to the infant and finally helps in throwing the removed wisps of hair safely away. The belief in days of yore being that evil spells could be cast on the child through the removed hair, it was important to wrap and spirit it away in such a manner that it was not accessible to ghoulish hands.

The operation ended with the *shikha,* a small tuft of hair, usually at the top of the head, being retained. A similar procedure was extant among the Chinese and the Tibetans. Even today, pandits all over India keep the tuft; even the laiety, especially in the north, with cropped hair and a western 'cut', still retain a small knot of hair at the rear, which they ostentatiously display when occasion demands and artfully camouflage at others!

Apart from conferring beauty and strength, *chudakarana* was also based on the belief that it conferred longevity. This is borne out from the averment of Sushruta, the ancient Ayurveda scholar and practitioner, who declared that there is a very vital spot on the top of the head, called *Adhipati,* Supreme Lord, marking the junction of two very crucial arteries that needed to be protected, and the *shikha* did this job.

The last of the childhood rites is *vidyaarambha,* also called *akshara abhyaasam,* literally the 'exercise of learning *aksharas,* the alphabets'; in Bengal it is called *haathe khudi.* Of interest is the term *niraksharakukshi* for the dumb-head unlettered in the alphabets!

It is customary to slot this ceremony in the *uttaraayana,* when the sun is in the northern hemisphere on an auspicious day which is identified, as is the case with all similar events, after evaluating the stars, day, *yogam,* an auspicious time-span (usually *siddha yogam* is preferred), and the *muhurtam.* Clothed in finery after the mandatory bath, the child faces the teacher who looks at him from the east. After propitiating Vighneswara or Ganesha, chief of the *ganas,* the heavenly hordes, Brihaspati, the *devaguru,* teacher of the celestials, and Saraswati, the Goddess of Learning, the teacher makes the child's fingers

ABOVE
The guru, Swami Chidananda Saraswati, initiates the brahmachari *at the* upanayana *ceremony at Parmarth Niketan, Rishikesh*

hold a golden, silver or other stylus and trace out a Divine name or a sentence on whole rice grains smeared with turmeric spread out on a salver of gold or silver or on a banana leaf, mouthing the words as they are formed.

The author recalls his own *akshara abhyaasam* when the first sentence he was guided to write was *Om namo Narayanayeti siddham*: Nothing moves save by Narayana's will. The omnipotence of the Divine was thus inculcated from the very beginning.

The teacher makes the child repeat the chosen words aloud for everyone to hear and thus the *vidyaarambha* is completed. The child offers salutations to the teacher, who receives his *dakshina,* fee, and assorted gifts for having officiated at the ceremony. There is festive rejoicing with sweets and other delicacies.

There is a remarkable parallel, too, among the Muslims. When the child is old enough to be initiated into the alphabets, the Maulana takes his tender fingers in his hand and guides him to write on a slate, *Bismillah-e-Rehman-e-Rahim*, Allah the Compassionate, the Merciful.

Thus the process which began with conception and birth culminates in the child being ready for the next step on the long and demanding road to familial and societal responsibilities and greater personal achievements in life.

4 | Upanayana — Ceremony of the Sacred Thread

From the starting point of togetherness between man and woman, united in the sacrament of *vivaha*, we regress to the era in a man's life that precedes matrimony; this is the period of studentship.

In the old days, education was not a matter of choice; resources and affordability were not factored into it. If a man has to enter upon the second of the *ashramas,* and launch out as a householder, capable of sustaining not only himself, his wife and offspring, but also others like the poor student, the infirm, the renunciate, he had to equip himself intellectually and practically, too. The Kshatriyas, warrior class, for instance, learnt at the *gurukula* not only the *Vedas, Puranas,* history, logic, philosophy,

music, dance, theatre but also archery and allied martial arts, the prime example being Drona teaching the Pandavas. The reference to 'resources' not being a constraint in education was made because it was only on completion of his *gurukulavasa,* stay in a residential school, that the student offered the *gurudakshina,* the preceptor's fee, that he could afford.

The years prescribed for the young man to devote himself to education, as a *brahmachari,* celibate, can also be likened to other forms of 'initiation' into life, e.g. circumcision in Islam, Baptism in Christianity, *bar mitzvah* in Judaism, *amrit samskara* in Sikhism and investiture of the *kushti* in Zoroastrianism. It is also akin to customs in certain communities in various parts of the world even today, prescribing tests of endurance and valour, periods of seclusion and bodily mutilation.

The initiation into the life of a student revolved around the *upanayana* ceremony, explained in the *Vedas* as *upanayamano brahmacharinam,* taking charge of a student. An elaborate ceremony preceded the formal acceptance of the child by the guru, whose qualifications were prescribed, along with the eligibility parameters of the student. Generally speaking, the guru was to be a Brahmin of a good family, devoted to the *Vedas* and fully committed to Vedic rituals. While these were *Veda*-specific, other traits that distinguished a guru were his observance of truth, ability to communicate and impart knowledge, spirit of universal compassion, courage of conviction, immaculate character and mastery of the *Vedas,* backed by unassailable faith in the Divine power. It is easy to see why all these were prerequisites, for in more senses than one, he was going to be the sole master of the student's life for the most impressionable period of 10 to 12 years. The parents' presence and influence not being there during this period of the child's life, it was the guru who had to discharge the dual role of parents and teacher.

With such a well-equipped and dedicated guru, it was virtually a rebirth for the student, for it was this ceremony of initiation that made him a *dvija,* twice born. To keep up the symbolism, it was held that the guru took the

LEFT
A cluster of young shishyas *(students/ disciples) at a modern* gurukula, *in idyllic surroundings*

child *raatrostrira udaro vibharti,* kept him unto [within] himself for three nights, like the foetus in the mother's womb, signifying that by his emergence from the guru he was reborn. When he completed his stint at the *gurukula* and sallied forth into the world, he emerged as *sarvaguna sampanna,* one endowed with all the desirable and splendid qualities of humankind. The symbolism was heightened by the stipulation that the child be dressed in yellow clothes the night preceding the ceremony, when he had to observe total silence too, symbolising the embryonic ambience and his relapse into the speechlessness from which he re-emerged into life and to speech.

The guru having been identified, the ceremony commenced. As with all celebrations and ceremonies, an auspicious day and time was selected, generally, during the months when the sun was in the northern hemisphere. In ancient times, seasons were earmarked for the *upanayana* of Brahmins (spring), Kshatriyas (summer), Vaishyas (autumn) and Rathakaras (monsoons). On the morning of the ceremony, the mother and child were given a lavish meal together to demonstrate *vaatsalya,* the mother's unique bond of affection for her child, as also to indicate that long years of anguished separation were to ensue before the acolyte returned home to the family and ate with the mother again. The mother's blessing was: "Fare thee well, my child! Go with thy belly full into the next stage of your life! And come back, fully fed with knowledge; my blessings go with thee!"

Then followed the shaving off of the hair, the ritual bath and the wearing of the *kaupina,* loin-cloth. All this was to signify that thenceforth, the blandishments of life like coiffure, fragrances and finery should mean nothing to him, for his entire being was to be aligned solely to the single-minded pursuit of knowledge. The guru gave him a simple *uttariya,* upper garment, dyed differently — saffron for Brahmins, madder for Kshatriyas and yellow for Vaishyas. These distinctions have yielded place now to yellow for all. Later, a small piece of deerskin was tied on to the *yajnopavita,* the sacred thread — a partial throwback to ancient times when the upper

garment was itself a deerskin, which the student evidently used at night to sleep on. The deerskin snippet tied to the sacred thread presaged intellectual lustre and pre-eminence. Then the boy was invested with a girdle originally made of grass, but now a twisted chord which helps hold the *kaupina* in place, as an essential accoutrement of purity and guarantor of celibacy.

Now for the most important part of the ceremony, the investiture of the *yajnopavita* which is made of handspun, hand-twisted yarn. The length of the yarn shall be 96 times the span of four fingers (between the little finger and the thumb), making up to the *brahmachari's* height. The four fingers point to the four states of existence — *jagra*, waking, *swapna*, dream, *sushupti*, dreamless sleep, followed by absolute oneness with the Supreme Brahman. The yarn is twisted into three strands and again into three separate strands and tied together in a *Brahmagranthi*, knot of Brahma, Vishnu and Shiva. The three strands stand for the three basic *gunas* or characteristics — *sattva*, the

ABOVE
The father and son, at the investiture of the yajnopavita *at* upanayana, *as the* pandit *guides*

real, *rajas,* passionate, and *tamas,* slothful or unillumined. They also remind one of the three *rnas,* debts, one owes to the *devas, rishis* and *pitrus,* i.e. celestials, sages and forefathers. In a later chapter we shall see these three receiving oblations during the *antim samskara, shraaddha* and *tharpan,* i.e. rituals and obeisance for the departed souls.

It is before the sacred fire that the guru invests the student with the *yajnopavita,* intoning the *mantra* from the *Paaraskara Grhya Sutra:*

> *Yajnopavitam paramam pavitram*
> *prajapateryatsahajam purastat*
> *ayushyamagriyam pratimuncha shubhram*
> *yajnopavitam bhalamastu tejah.*

May this sacred thread, which is purest of the pure, coeval with Prajapati, the first Being of the universe, confer on me longevity, hegemony, strength, scintillating [mind] and bring out the luminescence of knowledge.

Then the guru invests him with a *danda,* staff, usually made of a specified wood like the *palasa, udumbara* or *bilva* or *bel.* It was to remind the *brahmachari* that, as he was about to embark on a long voyage of self-improvement and self-discovery, the staff would protect him from all pitfalls and obstacles, as well as help him discharge miscellaneous duties enjoined on him by the guru, like tending to his herd or gathering fuel or fruits for the *gurupatni,* the guru's wife, and herbs from the forest. It must be remembered that a *brahmachari,* 'articled' as it were to the guru, was truly a bonded slave for the duration of his tutelage. No task was too menial or could be disregarded, for the whole process was one through which the young aspirant gathered nuggets of experience and knowledge that would serve him later in life.

Total concentration, thus, was on garnering knowledge, to the exclusion of all diversions and distractions. There is the very interesting story of a

guru who forbade his wife from serving *ghee* to his disciple — *ghee* being deemed to be an indispensable addition to the staple of lentils and rice. She was to serve him instead only bitter *neem* oil. One day, after 12 years of this regimen, the guru asked his wife to serve him *ghee*. Having tasted it, the student asked *guruma* (honorific for the guru's wife) as to why she had served him *neem* oil all those years. The guru told him thereupon that his education was complete; all these years he had not known nor cared that he was being served *neem* oil, for his mind was unflinchingly fixed on his studies. Now that his education was complete, he was again conscious of external things. There was nothing more that the guru could teach him.

At the investiture, the guru sanctified the student by pouring water into his cupped hands, with an appropriate invocation. Then he asked him to gaze at the sun, because it represented unswerving discipline and commitment to duty: *Karma sakshinamaadityam*, the sun witnessed all that

ABOVE
The guru flanked by his disciples in meditation before Aditya (sun), praying for total commitment to discipline and to duty

went on in the world. Thus, by purifying him with water and commanding him to worship the sun, the guru empowers him to receive the all-powerful *Gayatri mantra*. The *Gayatri mantra* is the pith of the whole exercise of the *upanayana samskara.*

Before the intoning and teaching of the *Gayatri mantra*, the guru touched the heart of his ward, invoking Prajapati (instead of Brihaspati, as in the otherwise self-same verse chanted during the *vivaha* ceremony), thus symbolically uniting him unto himself in a bond that was real and sincere, not based on expectations of reward or recompense. The adoption by the ward and the acceptance by the master have to be reciprocal, total and unqualified for the desired goal to be achieved.

Formally taking charge of his ward, the guru asked him his name, then, as to who his guru was. When the student pointed to the guru himself, the latter corrected him: "No, Indra and *agni* are thy teachers; and I follow" — indicative of the modesty of the guru and his summoning of the gods to take the acolyte in hand and impart all knowledge to him. Taking him around the sacred fire, he exhorted him to sip water and kindle the sacred fire with fuel. "Water is *amrit,* the elixir of life; work on, for work is worth, work is life; add fuel to the sacred fire, emblazon yourself with the light of knowledge; sleep not; do not die..."

The *Gayatri mantra*, the most sacred and the most popular of the Hindu *mantras*, deserves to be reproduced here:

> *Om bhur bhuvah suvaha*
> *tat savitur varenyam*
> *bhargo devasya dheemahi*
> *dhiyo yo nah prachodayaat.*

We meditate on the effulgence of the Creator (the sun), who is fit to be worshipped, who is the embodiment of knowledge and light, who cleanses all sins and dispels all ignorance. May He enlighten our intellect!

The *Gayatri mantra* starts with the primordial *pranava* (*Aum*) sound, which itself signifies that the individual soul is itself the Universal Soul (*So'ham* — the *jeevaatma* and the *Paramaatma* are but one). The *mahaa vyahritis* — *bhur, bhuvah* and *suvah* are the three spaces — earth, outer space and the ethereal regions beyond. *Savitr* is the sun, who is but the unparalleled energy of the Supreme Being, *Isvara*. *Bharga* is effulgence, *varenyam* is that which is fit to be worshipped. *Dheemahi* asks every one to meditate on that effulgence *dhi*, the intellect, leading to the realisation of that pure consciousness or full knowledge of the self.

This *mantra*, of salutations to and acknowledgment of the effulgence of the sun, is universal among Hindus. In the daily ritual of *sandhyavandana*, one is expected to recite the *mantra* 108, 32 and 64 times in the morning, noon and evening respectively. On the day following the *upakarma*, the annual renewal of the sacred thread, one is expected to do *Gayatri japa* by reciting the *Gayatri mantra* 1,008 times.

Thereafter the *brahmachari* kindled the sacred fire called *samid aadaana* reciting *mantras* replete with significance for the educational discipline which he had just embraced: this was the forerunner of the various fire rituals that he was expected to undertake through life. This was followed by his begging for alms. Usually he would go to his parents and close relatives, knowing they would not refuse! This was only to impress on him that he was still far from being self-supporting and that he would be dependent on charity for a long time. One may presume that it served also to kindle in him a lifelong disposition to be charitable to the needy.

The ceremony was rounded off with the *triraatra vrata*, penance of three nights: avoiding salted food, sleeping at night on bare ground, and keeping awake during the day. This was only to impress yet again on him the fact that the most exacting discipline was what he would be required to practice with relentless commitment in the long years that were to follow. When this *vrata* ended, the *medha janana*, the invoking of the intellect was performed, beseeching Goddess Medha to hone the intellect, fortify the memory and augment the power of retention.

After long years of the ward's *gurukulavasa* when the guru decided that he had imparted all the knowledge that he himself possessed and that the latter had absorbed all that he could, the *samaavartana* ceremony was held. This could be termed as the equivalent of the present-day convocation. The guru's convocation address consisted of these immortal words:

Sahanaa vavatu

sahanau bhunaktu

saha veeryam karavaavahai

tejasvinaa vadheethamastu

ma vidvishavahai.

What lofty, energising thoughts indeed: Let us together be protected; let us enjoy together; let us make learning more meaningful; let us achieve brilliance in our knowledge; let us do valorous things together, let us not be consumed by jealousy at the accolades that each one of us gets.

The idea of universal compulsory education, the choice of and criteria for the right guru, the absence of any stipulation as to fee, the essential qualities of the student, the sacrosanct bond between the guru and the disciple, the long years of tutelage at the gurukula, total subservience to the diktat of the guru in all matters, the implicit faith in the Universal Being conveying its blessings and endowing the student with the right attitudes and the right strengths and, finally, the convocation address which, in its pithiness contained unrivalled wisdom and peerless advice — these were the outstanding features of the ancient system of education of the young. Sadly, a very large part of it has become mere ritual, with its significance barely understood, and much less followed.

Before concluding this chapter, it would be of interest to see a kind of linked *samskara* in the Vaishnava *sampradaya*, Vaishnava tradition, called *samaasrayanam*, moving towards the protection of the guru. The guru of gurus being the Lord Himself, this ritual could be interpreted as total surrender to Vishnu Himself. For boys, *samaasrayanam* is *upanayanaantaram*, at the conclusion of the *upanayana* ceremony and for girls, it is *vivahaanantaram*, after marriage; thus there is no discrimination between the sexes.

After the appropriate invocations to the Divine and the necessary explanations to the candidates, the *shankha*, conch, and the *chakra*, the discus, which are the insignia of Vishnu, are branded by the *acharya*, guru, on the left and right shoulders of the candidate. The elements of the *pancha samskara*, five-fold rituals are: *tapam*, branding; *urdhva pundaram*, where the *acharya* applies the upstanding trident mark of the Vaishnava at 12 designated spots of the body, like the forehead, shoulders, arms, chest and the like; *dasya nama* where, as in the *upanayana*, another name is often conferred by the *acharya* with the suffix *daasa*, an obedient servant; *mantropadesam*, where the candidate is initiated into certain *mantras*, *stotrams* or excerpts from the *Puranas*; and *yagopadesha*, initiation into the rites of daily

ABOVE
Sadhguru Jaggi Vasudev of Isha Foundation, Coimbatore, with his disciples in natural environs

worship at home. The important element of *daasya nama* is the idea of total surrender unto the Lord — *Sharanaagathi Prapatti*.

This is but the echo of Shri Krishna's declaration in the *Bhagavad Gita*; *Maam ekam sharanam vraja*, I am the sole refuge; surrender thyself unto me! The Lord is my shepherd, I shall not want (*psalms*) is but another way of saying it!

The *Granth Sahib* has it too:

> *Kahere man chitve udham*
> *ja aahar har jiya pariya*
> *sayl paththar man jant upayaye*
> *taaka jijak aage kar dhariya.*

Oh mind! why are you agitated, when Hari himself is (ceaselessly) bothered about you? Do you not know that Hari has provided food even for creatures living encased in stone!

In the Islamic (and Sufi) tradition, there is the fascinating story of Haji Waris Ali Shah, Pir of Dewa Sharif (near Bara Banki in Uttar Pradesh). Someone asked the ageing Pir as to why he did not do the *namaaz* or keep the *zakat*. The Pir's laconic but peerless answer was; *Kono doori hoi to kuch kari!* Is there any distance between my Maker and me that I should do something (resort to these artifices)! Truly, no greater paradigm of total identification with and surrender to the Absolute can be found.

Should not all this make us wonder, what are we squabbling about?

ABOVE
The Guru Granth Sahib, *the holy book of the Sikhs, worshipped as the Divine*

5 | Sandhyavandana

The point of the ceremony of *upanayana* is not the ritualistic investiture of the *yajnopavita* but the imperative of making a *dvija* of the *brahmachari,* thus affirming his eligibility to receive the *Gayatri mantra. Sandhyavandana,* the concomitant of *upanayana,* is one of the seven *ahanikam,* daily rites, prescribed for *dvijas* of yore: *snaana,* bath, *sandhyavandana japa,* recitation or mental recapitulation of *mantras, homa,* offering to the sacred fire at home, *Veda paarayana,* reciting of the *Vedas, Deva puja,* worship of the Divine, and *atithi satkara,* offering of food to wayfarers, guests, indigents.

If there is one *mantra* that is of universal appeal, with no prohibitions even on women chanting it, it is the *Gayatri.* How does it derive its primacy? This is explained best by the simile, *Vipro vrikshah tasya moolam hi sandhya, moole chchinne pushpam phalam va.* The *dvija* is a tree; the *sandhya karma* is its root; if the root is cut off, where is the tree, the flower, the fruit? The *Vedas* assure that all kinds of benefactions flow from it.

What is interesting is that the ritual contains in itself the elements of *karma*, action, *bhakti*, devotion, *jnana*, knowledge and *yoga*. The *mantra* with the word *suryascha* is followed by *svaha*, denoting rite. *Arghya*, offering of water as an oblation, is an aspect of *bhakti*, coupled with veneration. *Pranayama*, breath control, is *yoga*. The phrase: *Asau adityah Brahma*, that sun, of knowledge, is Brahman, the seed of *jnana*.

The focus of worship is the Divine Shakti — worshipped as Gayatri, Savitri and Saraswati. At dawn, she is the virginal Gayatri as Brahmaswarupini, representing Brahma, the *Rigveda* and the trait of *rajas*. At noon, she is the mature Savitri as Rudrarupini, for Rudra (Shiva), the *Yajurveda* and *tamas*. At dusk she is the ageing Saraswati as Lakshmiswarupini, for the *Samaveda*, Vishnu and *sattva*.

A quick look now at the various steps of the *sandhyavandana:* the diurnal bath is the starting point. In almost all religions, ablutions in one form or another are a must. The *wazu* before the prayers in Islam and the washing of the hand at the sacred font at Church are prime examples, the idea being that purity of mind and heart follows cleanliness of the body, even if the act of washing is symbolic. The *Vedas* are categorical: 'All the *karmas* are to be performed only after a bath.' Donning clean clothes, one sits facing the east and commences the ritual by sipping thrice a little portion of water held in the cupped right palm, intoning three names of Vishnu — Achyuta, Ananta and Govinda. Wiping his lips, he then lightly touches with his fingers various parts of the body (termed *anga nyaasa*), starting with the cheeks and ending with the heart and the top of the head to invoke the *navagrihas,* nine planets, and 12 names of Vishnu — Keshava, Naarayana (cheeks), Maadhava, Govinda (eyes), Vishnu, Madhusudana (nostrils), Trivikrama and Vaamana (ears), Sridhara, Hrishikesa (shoulders), Padmanaabha (navel) and

Damodara (top of the head). There is a beautiful symbolism here — repeating the Lord's name intensely purifies all the functional organs and enables each one of them to concentrate on Him and, of course, on *loka kshema*, the weal of the world.

The *sankalpa*, declaration of the objective follows, and then *praanayaama*, where the breath is taken in through the left nostril, *pooraka*, holding it, or *kumbhaka*, and, expelling it through the right nostril, *rechaka*. The *pranaayaama mantra* is in four parts — in honour of the primordial *Aum*

ABOVE
The guru with his disciples doing the sandhya havan *on the banks of the* Ganga

Traditions & Rituals   **51**

(*pranava mantra*), the seven *vyahritis* (*bhoor, bhuvah, suvah, mahah, janah, tapah* and *satya*), the associated *rishis, chandas* and *devatas*, and finally *Gayatri siras; Omaapo jyotiraso amrtam brahma bhur bhuvahsuvarom.* The last is a crisp enunciation of the *swarupa*, form, of the *Paramaatma*, Supreme Being, as water, effulgence, *rasa*, essence, and *amrita*, ambrosia, embodying the powers of creation, sustenance and rhythm.

Then occurs further sprinkling of water on the head, called *marjanam*, for not only purification but for invoking the latent energy that water contains. One takes in drops of water again, invoking *suryascha*, for the sun, *apah punantu*, for the cleansing water, and *agnischa* for Agni, respectively at morning, noon and dusk. It is of interest to know what, for instance, the morning mantra says: 'Let Surya (and other gods) absolve me of sins that I may have committed out of anger, of the sins I might have committed last night, in my mind, through speech, through hands and feet and stomach or the male organ or from any other sin that might inhere in me. I offer myself (*svaahaa*) unto the liberating heat and fire of the sun'.

After another brief *marjanam, arghya* is offered unto the *navagrahas* and the 12 manifestations of Vishnu.

Gayatri is then formally invoked and distinctly split into five parts, the *mantra* is chanted, as stated already, at least 108, 64 and 32 times, morning, noon and evening respectively. It is believed that this *mahamantra*, the mightiest of *mantras*, consisting of 24 syllables was what inspired Valmiki to compose the *Ramayana* in 24,000 stanzas; Tyagaraja, one of the Carnatic musical trinity, to compose 2,400 *kritis*, compositions, in praise of Rama, and Jayadeva to compose 24 *ashtapadis*, hectametres, in inspired delineation of the divine love of Krishna and Radha.

Gayatri japa over, the ritual is brought to a close through various *upastana mantras*,* invoking and imploring the blessings of gods and *rishis*, through the worship of the four directions, offering one's respects to Yama, God of Death, to rivers like the Narmada — the concept of deference to and care of ecology may be noted and finally, to Surya and Narayana (Vishnu). The ritual ends with the offering of *shaastanga namaskara*, prostrating on the ground, with eight *angas*, parts of the body touching the ground, signifying the utmost humility in the attitude of *sharanaagati*, to avow: 'Thy feet are my only refuge!' and the asking of forgiveness for any inadvertent omissions and commissions that might have occurred during the entire ritual by default of *manah*, mind, *vaak*, speech, *kaaya*, body/limbs, *indriyas*, organs, or *prakriti*, natural inclinations. This is again a reiteration of the imperative of the elimination of *ahambhava*, the 'I factor'.

ABOVE
An installation of the navagrihas *(the nine planets), usually in temples*

LEFT
A young brahmachari *offering* arghya *during* sandhyavandana *at the Ganga, Kashi*

---

* *Mantras* chanted at the end (mainly) of the *trikala sandhyavandana*, as also at the end of some other rituals

6 | The Other Ashramas

In his *People of India,* Abbé Dubois (1817) wrote:

"The Brahmans divide their progress through life into four stages: the first is that of a young man of the caste, when he has been invested with the triple cord (*brahmachari*). The second is when the Brahman becomes a married man. In this condition, and particularly when he is the father of children, he obtains the appellation of *grihasta.* He reaches the third stage when, being satiated with the world, he resolves to retire into the desert, with his wife, and then he receives the name of *vanaprasta* (an inhabitant of the wilderness). The fourth and the last stage is that of the *sanyasin,* at which he arrives when he devotes himself to a life of solitude,

ABOVE
*Devotees at a
satsang (colloquium
on spiritual matters)
between a guru and
his followers*

with no wife; and in a still higher degree of seclusion than the *vanaprasta*."

We have, in the chapter on *upanayana*, looked at the *brahmachari's* life. A brief look at the other three *ashramas* also will help in understanding the organisation of an individual's life in ancient times, including not only rituals but also the creation and observance of traditions, alongside their implications for the individual as well as the community. The *grihasta*, householder, is undoubtedly the pivot, since he is the one best equipped to take care of the *brahmachari* and the *sanyasin*, in addition to looking after his own wife, children and even the extended family.

This multi-faceted responsibility is inherent in the five *yajnas* (literally, sacrifices) prescribed for him. *Devayajna, rishiyajna, pitruyajna, bhutayajna* and *atithiyajna* (also called *narayajna* or *purushayajna)* are sacrifices or offerings to the gods, sages, manes, humanity and guests. Homage to the gods is in the form, usually, of daily *pujas* to the deities, *ksheratana,* visits to temples and *teertha yatra,* bathing in holy rivers and seas, paying obeisance to the gods on special occasions like Makara Sankranthi for the sun, or *asvattha pradakshina,* circumambulation, of the *peepul* tree, on Amavasya, new moon day, if is falls on *somavara,* Monday. The *peepul* tree is hailed as a sacred tree whose roots, stem and crown are inhabited respectively by the Holy Trinity, Brahma, Vishnu and Shiva.

Rishiyajna is obeisance to the sages in gratitude for their having imparted knowledge. Homage to *rishis* also signifies deference to one's lineage, their names being invoked when one prostrates before elders and recounts one's pedigree, going on to mention the *gotra* and *pravara* to which one belongs and ending with the mention of one's name, such as, *Vaidyalinga sarma naamaaham asmi bhoh,* I, Vaidyalinga Sarma, prostrate before thee and touch the ground in front of thee. 'Vaidyalinga' was the name conferred on the author at his *upanayana.*

One may now look at the *sraaddha* ceremony under the classification *pitruyajna,* since it is to be performed by both the *brahmachari* and the *grihasta* as a mark of remembrance, love and regard for one's deceased parents (the widower, if he has no sons, has to do the *sraaddha* for his wife). *Sraaddha* is done once a year — a day of the *pitrus* being deemed to be equal to one year of the living. In a manner of speaking, it is thus the equivalent of daily remembrance of the departed. Since this is an act of faith, however, *sraaddha* has to be performed with *sraddha,* absolute faith.

ABOVE
Aswatta (peepul) tree, considered an object of worship, as the habitat of the Hindu Trinity

RIGHT
Bhairav at Kedarnath which, along with Badrinath, ranks among the holiest of Himalayan dhams, temples — a symbol of man's faith

We have seen that, apart from the *yajnas* towards the *pitrus*, the *grihasta* has to take care of all living beings. In the olden days, the householder performed the daily rituals of *agnihotram* and *vaisvadevam*, tending the *gaarhyapatyaagni*, the domestic fire which he had to tend to from the day of his marriage, and cooking the consecrated rice offering for the *Visvedevas*, a section of the *pitrus*. After completing the rituals and taking food, the householder had to step out of his house and hail all four directions loudly, asking if there were any guests waiting to be fed. This also ties up with the dictum '*atithi devo bhava*', the guest is God; but even He ranks last, after mother, father and guru — *Maatru devo bhava, pitru devo bhava, acharya devo bhava, atiti devo bhava.*

The penultimate stage, *vanaprasta* marks the period in one's life when, after a person has fulfilled one's responsibilities as a householder and father, got his children married off and seen them settled in life, he retires as a recluse, with his wife, to the *vana,* forest, and living off herbs, roots and fruits of the forests, spends all his time in contemplation of the Divine, and reflecting on the verities of life. Incidentally, this gives a clue to the ecological certainty that there were enough forests in those days to accommodate *vanaprastas,* a far cry from todays vanishing forest cover.

Vanaprasta may well be deemed as probation for the next (and last) *ashrama*, that of the *sanyasin,* in the sense that after having given up as a *vanaprasta* all family links (except for the spouse) and all material allures, a man had already travelled far on the path of renunciation, all he had to do was to give up his wife, too, at this point! He shaves off his head, casts off his *yajnopavita*, does *atma sraaddha*, his own *sraaddha.* Now on he is 'dead' to the world. He takes a dip in a holy river and, casting off his clothes, rises from the waters to don *kaashaya vastra,* ochre robes, and is ordained by his guru, who is himself a senior *sanyasin.*

Once ordained, the *sanyasin* is expected to sever all links with the family, especially the wife (that was)! He has to have no fixed abode, usually not staying at any place for more than *triratra vasa,* stay of three nights. According to the strictest code, he is not supposed to ask for alms from more than three households, and that to just once a day, as he intones, *Bhavati bhikshaam dehi,* Oh respected lady! Be pleased to give me some food. He is to control his palate with relentless firmness, and take in the same bowl whatever is offered to him thus, be it rice or vegetables or sweets; in short, no indulgence of the palate either! In fact, *karapaatri sanyasins* do not even use a bowl; they take the food offered to them only in their cupped palms.

The only period in the year that the *sanyasin* may stay at one place for more than three nights is *chaaturmaasya,* the four-month period of the monsoons. Otherwise, the *sanyasin* is a *parivraajaka: Paritah vrajati iti parivraajaka,* wandering round and round, hence *parivraajaka.* Equally with the Hindu *sanyasins,* the Jain *munis* and Buddha *bhikkus,* monks, observe this as a period of meditation, reflection and dissemination.

The reasons for this practice are many: insects of all kinds which abound during rains are thus saved from being crushed under the feet of the wandering monk; it saves him from being attached to one place or becoming used to one particular community of people or one set of hospitable persons at one preferred location; the third is that this being earmarked period of penance and meditation, rooted as he is to one spot, the *sanyasin* is enabled without distraction and disquiet, to contemplate Brahman; and finally, it enables the lay population of the area to gather around to listen to him and benefit from his own *Brahma vichara,* inquiry into the Brahman, and ways of comprehending the nature of the Infinite. The itinerant monk becomes a 'tenure' preacher during this period!

There are prescriptions and proscriptions as to food — it may be added at this point, equally for the monks and the laity — that one should eat and one should avoid during periods like the monsoons, pointing at once to the tremendous medical knowledge of our ancients, the respect they had for the human body and the body-mind nexus when they declared: *Sharira madhyam*

ABOVE
An aged sanyasin
with his danda
*(staff), at the Sankara
Mutt, Kashi*

khalu dharma sadhanam, indeed the body is the medium for the pursuit of *dharma.*

The highlight of *chaaturmaasya* for the Hindu *sanyasins* is the Vyaasa *puja,* Sage Vyaasa being revered as the *adiguru* (the progenitor). It is celebrated in other similar religions as Buddhapurnima, Gurupurnima and Gurupurab.

The exalted position accorded to the *sanyasa ashrama* in Hinduism can be seen from the salutation chanted in honour of a *sanyasin.* The very beginning is evocative: *Na karmanaa na prajayaa dhanena tyage naike amrtatva maanasuh,* neither action nor progeny can confer the certitude of salvation as can sacrifice, the reference being to the *sanyasin's* total abandonment of all ties, pleasures and desires.

If *swarga,* heaven, and the *pitruloka* are the desiderata of the ordinary mortal, that of the *sanyasin* is the attainment of the *Brahmaloka* and *Brahmasayujya,* attaining the attributes of Brahman itself. Thus the last rites of the *sanyasin* have also to be different from those of the householder. The ritual in this case, called the *Brahmamedha,* consists of the body being laid in a trench in the earth; often the body is lowered into it in a seated posture, with the *karapatra,* bowl, on his belly and his *kamandal,* water pot, in his right hand. At present, the custom, as delineated in *Yati Samskara,* a *Smriti* text detailing the sacraments pertaining to a *yati (sanyasin)* is to break the skull with a consecrated coconut, in the belief that it is the hole right atop the skull known as *Brahmarandhra,*

through which the soul of the *Brahmajnani* ascends heavenward. No further rites or continuing obsequies are performed for a *yati*. Be it noted too that it is customary to speak, not of a *sanyasin's mrityu*, death, but Swamiji attained *siddhi* (*samadhi*), realisation. As a corollary, the day of his *siddhi* is celebrated each year as the day, not of the *sraaddha*, but as of the *aaraadhana*, act of worship.

It is interesting, before we conclude, to see what Adi Sankara has to say in his *Bhaja Govindam*:

ABOVE
Antim aarti *being offered to Swami Chinmayananda before his* bhoosamadhi *(internment) as ordained for a* sanyasin, *Sidhbari, Himachal Pradesh*

> *Jatilo mundi lunchita kesaha kaashayambara bahukrta veshaha,*
> *pashyannapi cha na pashyati mudho, hyudara nimittam bahukrta veshaha.*

There are those who masquerade in a beard or with a head shaven or hairs plucked out and in ochre robes, all these just to satiate the stomach and assuage the pangs of hunger.

The unity of belief (and exposition) among religions is further borne out by this declaration of Guru Nanak:

> *Jog na kintha jog na dande jog na basm,*
> *anjan mahe niranjan rahiye jog jugat iv paiye.*

Union is achieved not through wearing tattered clothes, carrying a staff or smearing oneself with holy ash; it is achieved only by remaining pure amidst the impurities of life.

Indeed, Adi Sankara and Guru Nanak had foreknowledge of some of the *sadhus* and *sanyasins* of our days!

Finally, let it not be taken that it is imperative to traverse the three preceding ashramas before entering upon the life of a *sanyasin*! When Adi Sankara was asked how he could have done so, his classic rejoinder, according to the *Jalabala Upanishad* was: *Yat ahar eva vrajet tad ahareva pravraje,* the moment you attain *vairaagya,* state of total renunciation, enough to renounce this world, at that very moment, tarry not but go ahead and renounce it!

7 | Antim Samskaras — Funeral Rites

On his birth, man arrives from the unknown at the perceivable; death marks his departure from the known to the unknown. Just as a host of rites, in the Hindu system, mark his journey from his creation as an embryo in a womb, it is not surprising that a whole set of rites mark his cremation and thereafter. Other observances and practices mark the Islamic and Christian tradition as also in others, in ancient times like the old Greek, Roman, Egyptian eras upon the happenstance of death.

One who has lived by and for *dharma* all his life, need have no fear of death.

Realised souls like Bhishma had even the power to will the precise time of their death. Not for Bhishma the chanting of the Lord's name only on the deathbed, for the likes of him live in God, live with God all their lives.

Notwithstanding the quality of the life that one may have led, and whatever be one's state of self-realisation, the obsequies and funereal rites are as inescapable as death is inevitable. As we have seen, even the *sanyasin* is not exempt, although, in the Hindu system, he is not cremated but buried, and with no extended rituals; and his annual *sraaddha* is celebrated not as such but as *aaradhana*. The ancients believed that through the rites of the living, earth is won; and through the *antim samskaras,* last rites, the very heaven. Till the rites are completed, it is believed that the departed lingers on as mere *preta*, corpse, and it is these *samskaras* that free him finally from this world and make him eligible to be with the departed ancestors.

In the olden days, longevity was more the rule than the exception, as evidenced by the celebration of *shashtiabdhapoorthi* and *shatabhishekam,* the sixtieth and eightieth birthdays; *durmaranam,* untimely or non-felicitous death (due to sad and inauspicious causes) was practically unknown. Thus it was that, as death was nigh, the person was moved from his bed to the earth, with his head to the south, the abode of Yama, the God of Death. Sacred hymns, or verses from the *Bhagavad Gita,* the *Ramayana* or the *Bhagavata* are chanted so that the departing soul's ears ring with the name of the Lord and his or her way to heaven is strewn with roses, as it were. For did not Adi Sankara say that, at the point of death; *Nahi nahi rakshati dukrunjkarane,* knowledge of grammar will not help one! It is only Govinda's name that will.

As part of the rituals (or customs) for the dying: most Indian households keep small copper pots of *Ganga jal,* Ganga water, worshipped at home through the years; and invariably, a drop of the holy water therefrom is spooned on to the dying lips.

In Adi Sankara's words again, beginning with *Bhagavad Gita kinchit adeeta*

Ganga jalalava kanikaa pitha...., he who has even a nodding acquaintance with the *Bhagavad Gita,* sipped a little of the water of the Ganga and worshipped Murari (Vishnu) even in passing, his deliverance is assured.

Thus purified by the holy Ganga and reassured by the Lord's name, life ebbs away. The closest relative, usually the eldest son, or a grandson or other near relative, addresses the corpse and asks it to give up the old clothes and remember the sacrifices performed and the *dakshina* and other gifts that it had bestowed on *pandits* and others in its lifetime. The body is washed and covered in one piece of unbleached cloth, leaving just the head uncovered. Then it is placed (usually) on a bamboo bier. The funeral cortege sets out for the *samasaana,* cremation ground, led by the eldest son (or any other as stated above), who carries an earthen pot with fire (usually a smouldering cowdung cake). In the south, there is the tradition of the grandson carrying a flaming torch lit with a *ghee*-soaked cloth, called *pandam* in Tamil. In the north, it is customary for the mourners who accompany the bier to chant; *Ram nama satya hai,* the one truth is Sri Rama's name.

On reaching the cremation ground (it may be noted that babies and children below two are not cremated, but buried), the body is taken off the bamboo bier, with the bonds over the thumbs being loosened, and placed on a mound of logs, in which it is customary to include at least a small sandalwood piece. There is usually the gift of a cow, symbolically termed *vaitarani,* envisaged as someone who keeps company with the departed to smoothen his passage across the mythical River Vaitarani before quitting the earth. After appropriate chants, a handful of rice is put into the mouth of the corpse by the chief mourner and other close relatives. This signifies the end of the preliminaries.

Then the funeral fire is lit, first with the fire brought by the chief mourner, and is fed with other combustibles till the flames burst forth and engulf the body. This is symbolic of the concept of Agni, the God of Fire, being the conveyor of the departed to the gods. A *Rig Vedic* prayer

LEFT
Pitru tharpan, *oblations to the manes, at the Ganga, Kashi, mark the* pracheenaaveeti, *the* yajnopavita *on the right shoulder, on the man, second from right*

beseeches *agni,* not to cause pain to the body nor scatter it about nor incinerate it to cinders but to convey the spirit to the ancestors. With other invocations, various organs of the body are also offered to various gods — like the eyes (sight) to *surya* and breath to *akasha,* atmosphere. Purification follows, with their sprinkling themselves with the water poured from an odd number of jars into three small pits to the north of the pyre (this is called *kuzhi tharpanam,* in Tamil Nadu). Then they walk away without looking back.

They then proceed to bathe in a river or stream nearby, if there is one, in a ritual called *udaka karma,* the rite of offering water to the departed. Those invested with the sacred thread wear it at this point in the *niveeti* style, i.e. instead of it resting on the left shoulder, it is worn as a garland. Facing the south, they offer handfuls of water to the departed soul in his name. Returning home, they again purify themselves with a bath, usually before setting foot inside.

However, the *asaucha,* pollution caused by the death, lasts for 10 days among the close relatives. This is evidently to indicate to the world that the family, bereft of a near and dear person, is suffering from intense grief and sorrow, forswearing jollity and even the performance of the daily *pujas* (at the altar at home) and other auspicious rites during this period. There is also a convention, especially in south India that if one does not make a condolence call on the bereaved family within the first 10 days, one has to wait for a year. There is also the convention that one does not go to the bereaved household to condole on Saturdays and Mondays. Also, on the day of the death, no fire is lit at home, even for cooking. It is a time-honoured custom for neighbours and relatives living close- by to cater to the immediate members of the bereaved family by bringing food from their own homes.

The *asti sanchayana,* collection of the remains of the funeral pyre, is usually on the third day. The bones are collected to the accompaniment of

verses, the symbolic support of which is that they reassemble in the other world, taking on a new shape. They are washed and collected in an urn and are usually taken to and immersed in the Ganga or other holy rivers.

Easy to see is the particular merit in choosing the Ganga for the immersion. As the *sutra* has it, if the *asti* is consigned to the Ganga: *Yugaanaam tu sahasraani tasya swarge bhaved gathihi*, the one whose bones are immersed in the Ganga lives in *swarga* (heaven) for thousands of aeons. No wonder then that dear relatives from across the country and continents travel thousands of kilometres just to consign the *asti* into it at Varanasi or Hardwar. demonstrably care about. Of course, there is also the basic belief, *kaashyaante maranaan muktihi*, if one dies in Varanasi, salvation is assured. The author recalls his mother's admonition that, if she were to fall seriously ill and need hospitalisation, she should not be taken to any hospital which was beyond the boundaries marked by the Varuna and the Asi rivers (hence the name Varanasi).

There are daily offerings thereafter for the departed, *pinda daanam*, usually consisting of rice balls and sesame, visualised as contributing to the reassembling of various parts of his body into a whole. On the twelfth day, *sapindikarana* directed towards uniting the departed with the manes is performed, signifying that the deceased has ceased to exist as a *preta,* corpse, and has joined the assemblage of ancestors.

The *asaucha* period ends on the thirteenth day, when *punyahavachanam*, the final purificatory ritual is performed and the house sprinkled with water that has been consecrated. A feast is held, to which relatives and close friends are invited.

This marks the end of the funeral rituals, which, in the opinion of some scholars, are based largely on primitive beliefs about life and death, the next world being, in the estimation of Dr Rajbali Pandey, "nothing but a replica of this earth, and the needs of the dead are the same as those of the living." In other words, it is tantamount to saying goodbye for, one day, sooner or later, will not the living go to meet the dead in the 'next world'?

8 | Traditions

Traditions basically consist of actions and practices based on ancient lore and custom. In a more significant way, however, they are of phenomenal and continuing import to life and living, as they stem from the intrinsic ethos and culture that are essentially 'man-making'.

In the first category are traditions like keeping and worshipping the *tulsi* plant at home, usually installed in the open courtyard in a small but typical structure of time-honoured design. The leaf of the *tulsi* plant, thus worshipped, as Tulsidevi, the favourite of Vishnu, is not to be used in *puja,* since it has been the object of *puja* itself.

One should not sniff at or smell flowers picked for *puja*, nor use flowers that have fallen on the ground, except a flower like the *parijata (harsingar* in Hindi). This tree is a prolific bloomer and it is difficult to pluck the blossoms individually.

Flowers and other offerings to the deity are always carried in the right hand, the left being considered *ashuddha*, impure. In fact, giving anything to another with the left hand is considered insulting; it is *de rigeur* to offer to and receive gifts from another and to make offerings to deities and receive *prasaad* (flowers, sacred ash, *kumkumam* or eats offered to the deity) with both hands, as along with them goes the *prana*, vital energy.

Flowers having no fragrance or having a foul odour are never to be offered to the deity, nor flowers that grow on a thorny plant unless they are white or sweet-scented. Only *ghee* and select oils are to be used in votive lamps.

One should not sit in front of an elder with one's legs stretched towards him or her, nor indeed, towards a shrine or a temple. One should always show respect to an elder by prostrating to (or, in the north Indian tradition, by touching the feet of) the latter at the first meeting on each occasion as well as when taking leave. The author's grandfather had a pragmatic explanation for this. As you prostrate before him, he has perforce to say, in the hearing of everyone present, *deergaayushmaan bhava*, may you live long!, even if he harbours a thought which is totally contrary to his expressly articulated blessing. The dark thought in his mind is thus cancelled out by his outspoken blessing!

In south India, the ground in front of the home is swept early in the morning, sprinkled with water, daubed with cowdung and then decorated with rice-flour in beautiful patterns called *kolam*. Parsimonious households use stone-powder, but I recall that to my mother this was anathema, since it was not edible and the whole purpose of using rice-flour was to provide food to the army of ants and birds that would gather around! Similarly, a

LEFT
Puja samagri —
*flowers, fruits,
coconuts, betel
leaves,* deepa (ghee
or oil lamp), incense,
chandan *(sandal),*
sindhura
*(vermillion) — all
essential ingredients
for the* puja

lamp (using oil and a cotton wick) is lit at the front door purposely kept ajar in the evening, while the rear door is kept shut; this is to welcome into the home Sridevi or Lakshmi, the Goddess of Prosperity, and to prevent her mean and malefic counterpart (Moodevi, in Tamil) from sneaking in through the backdoor, apart, of course, from the mosquitoes and rodents breeding in the rear gutter!

There are other interesting prescriptions and traditions in respect of behaviour at mealtimes. We have seen that the *atiti*, is to be fed first. The exceptions are a married girl who has not yet joined her husband, an unmarried girl, a sick woman and a pregnant woman — these can be fed even before the guests. There are other do's and don'ts too, such as: one must not eat at *sandhyakalam*, dusk, nor clad in wet clothes, nor while standing in water, nor while lying on one's back or reclining on a couch, nor eat food that has been seasoned with salt after it has been cooked and nor eat curd at night.

One is not to cut nails on Fridays or after lamps have been lit in the evening; it is also forbidden to bite or pinch away nails. One

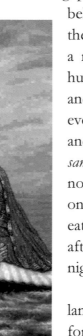

ABOVE
Vishnu as
Ananthasayani,
reclining amid
ksheerasagara
(ocean of milk) on the
thousand-headed
Adishesha, *with*
Lakshmi *at his feet*

must not sew at night. Sewing, clipping, scissoring and similar operations are not to be undertaken lightly by pregnant women during *chandra/surya grahanams*, lunar and solar eclipses, for the belief is that, if by accident the woman pricks or cuts herself, the child will be born with a defect, like harelip or cleft palate. The tradition also is that no cooked food shall be retained during the eclipse nor consumed after the eclipse is over, as it is considered unhealthy due to invisible contamination. In fact, small pieces of the *darbha* grass are kept even in the containers holding dry rations, so that they do not get affected by the eclipse.

There are specified periods each day of the week when travel is not to be commenced, nor auspicious and happy events performed or celebrated. The worst is the *rahukalam*, the period of Rahu, the malefic one among the *navagrahas*, nine planets, which stretches for an hour and a half each day lasting, for example, from half past seven to nine in the morning on Mondays, nine to half past ten on Saturdays, and so on. To be totally avoided is the *rahukalam* on Sunday, between 4.30 and 6.00 in the evening.

There are good and bad *yogams*, auspicious time intervals, too: *siddha* and *amrita yogams* are good, while *marana yogam* is to be totally avoided. Similarly, the *muhurtam* which, as we have seen, is the precise time-span for the conduct and culmination of any auspicious or gala event is to be chosen with meticulous care, examples being a wedding or laying the foundation of a new house, *griha pravesam*, the ceremonially entering and occupying for the first time a newly-built or rented home. The last cited is a ritualistic variant of housewarming, one may say! The star, the planet, the *yogam* and the *kalam* (both referring to specified time-slots in a day when actions may be initiated or must be avoided) are among the most significant factors in the involved calculations for deciding on the *muhurtam*.

Travel in certain directions is to be avoided on specified days. For instance, travel eastward is not undertaken on Mondays and Saturdays, southward on Thursdays and so on.

One should not sleep with one's head to the north, the theory being that *Yamaloka*, the abode of Yama, the God of Death, is in the south and one should not indicate his readiness for the final journey before the appointed time!

There are sundry (but interesting) traditions too — like the taboo on stepping over a rope to which a calf or a cow is tethered. After a bath, one must not shake one's head to get rid of the water drops. One should not point out a rainbow to others. Trees never to be cut are the *bel, peepul,* tamarind, fig, lemon and banyan. One should not spit or cast used flowers, fruits or food into water/river and make it impure, or gaze at one's reflection in water or in a vessel containing oil. Most interesting is that when one sneezes, those nearby are to say, *shatam jeeve,* live to be a hundred, which is precisely the Western custom of 'Bless you'!

There is also the tradition of reciting a very simple prayer first thing in the morning on waking up. Looking at one's upturned palms and fingers, one chants:

Karagre vasateh Lakshmih
kara madhye Saraswati.
Karamoole tu Govinda
prabhate karadarshanam.

The prayer is to Lakshmi, the presiding deity of prosperity who lives at the tips of the fingers, and to Saraswati, the Goddess of Learning, whose habitat is the palms, while Govinda (Vishnu) lives at the root of the palms. This is to say: Whatever we may desire, be it knowledge or wealth or cognition of *Paramaatma,* it is all in our own hands. What an exquisite thought, the echo of what the *Gita* exhorts one to do, *uddharedaatmanaatmaanam,* raise yourself through your own efforts!

There are lots of prescriptions and proscriptions too, when one sets out of the home; of course, some of them may sound ludicrous in this day and age! Being accosted by a single Brahmin, one whose hair and body are smeared with oil, a black cat, an oil monger, a barber or a *sanyasin* — all these are considered ill omens. Seeing a *sumangali,* a woman whose husband is alive, or a washerman carrying washed clothes on a donkey and, not seeing but hearing a donkey's bray are all good omens! If a bell rings when one is about to start something new or auspicious, that endeavour promises to be a success; a sneeze, the opposite!

RIGHT
A rudraksha mala for Hindu's japa— *corresponding to the rosary of the Christian, the* tasbih *of the Muslim and the* sumirana *of the Sikh*

Cooking for a *sraaddha* is to be done wearing wet clothes, after a bath. Certain vegetables are taboo for the *sraaddha* — like root vegetables, tomato, drumstick, cauliflower, beans and cabbage; others are preferred, like jackfruit, banana and snake gourd, along with curry leaves. *Til laddus*, sweet sesame balls, are prescribed, possibly because of the association of sesame with comestibles for the manes. Not refined sugar but *gur*, jaggery, is to be used. Red chillies are taboo too; instead black pepper is to be used. It is also the tradition to give up one's favourite leaf, vegetable or fruit after performing the *sraaddha* at Gaya; of course, many try the easy way out by giving up the banyan leaf, *karela,* bitter gourd (*Momordica charantia),* and the *jamun,* Indian blackberry (*Eugenia jambolana*). The first you can't eat, the second is too bitter for most and the third is only a seasonal fruit which one can very well do without!

There are other traditions which have taken on the form of festivals and observances, like the Varalakshmi Vratam in the south and Karva Chauth in the north — both essentially for women praying for the longevity of their husbands. Interestingly, however, the former is not observed in all homes; the daughter-in-law has to observe it only if the custom exists in her mother-in-law's home.

Rakhi (Raksha Bandhan) is so popular in north India demonstrating the bonds of enduring love between sister and brother that it needs no elaboration. In the south, this day is marked out as the day for the renewal of the *yajnopavita,* followed by the *Gayatri japa* the next day when, after the proper *sankalpa,* declaration of objective or desideratum, the *Gayatri mantra* is chanted 1,008 times. This is to atone (partially) for not having been regular in doing the *Gayatri japa* during the year gone by.

The tradition of *aswattha pradakshina,* circumambulation, is usually undertaken by women. The tradition also abounds, throughout India, one may add, regardless of religious affiliation, of taking a vow to visit a shrine or making a substantial offering to one's favourite deity. Such vows, termed *mannaths (*or in Tamil *venduthalai),* are to solicit Divine intervention for being blessed with a child, or cure of a severe illness, or the marriage of the daughter, or outstanding success in an examination, or a good job or an office promotion for oneself or the offspring, or the solution of a particularly intractable business or family problem.

Traditions are the salt and spice of life. The traditions of respect to elders, particularly the parents and the guru, hospitality, regard for women, loyalty and friendship, compassion, love and mercy, honesty, concern for ecology and environment, kindness to animals, equality of mankind, respect for and non-deviation from justice and, most of all, the acknowledgement of the intrinsic equality of all religions, are what can rightfully and legitimately be called our own inalienable traditions. They are no more and no less than universally valid parameters of existence, all directed towards leading a noble and enlightened life.

It is time we looked at larger aspects of traditions — as are not mere 'observances' or 'imposts'; they are verily the Indian way of life down the centuries. To start with is respect for elders. It is significant that 'mother' has universal pride of place, and Islam is no exception. On being asked again and again as to who should be venerated most, the Prophet repeatedly said 'the mother'. Only the sixth time, did He say: 'And then, the father'.

There are legends galore in this context: Shravan Kumar carried his blind parents all over the pilgrim centres of the land, in baskets slung over his shoulders; Pundarik, while ministering to his aged parents' needs in his home tossed a brick out and asked Lord Vital himself to wait till he was through with *seva*, service to his parents; and Rama abandoned a kingdom because of the diktat of his father at the behest of a scheming stepmother.

The tradition of respect for women is an ancient one too — alas increasingly violated (in more senses than one today). The wife was the *saha-dharmini* — one who assists in the discharge of the husband's *dharma*.

Hospitality has been not merely a tradition but a way of life. There is the legend of Adi Sankara who, as a *brahmachari*, sought alms from a very poor lady, whose husband and she had no food at home even for themselves. But she had one *amla*, cape gooseberry (*Emblica officinalis*) which she gladly offered to Sankara, who was so overwhelmed that he composed on the spot *Kanakadhaarastavam* (Ode to the Shower of Gold). Lo and behold, there was a veritable shower of gold *amlas* from heaven! Such was the power of hospitality and compassion.

It is useful not only to recall, in these days of communal conflagrations and demoniacal fratricides, but also to start practising anew the tradition of compassion and universal love. An enunciation by Tulsidas is succinct but vivid:

> *Daya dharma ka mool hai paap mool abhiman,*
> *tulsi daya na chhodiye jab lag ghat mein pran.*

Compassion is the root of *dharma*, just as sin is that of pride; do not give up compassion so long as there is breath in thy body, says Tulsi.

The tradition of compassion, though, is not the exclusive trait of the Hindu or the Sufi. The equality of humankind and the universal need for all-embracing compassion is reflected in the *Granth Sahib* too:

> *Brahmgyaani sada samdarsi*
> *Brahmgyaani ki dristi amrit barsi.*

One who is blessed with total awareness of the Universal Soul looks at humankind with unvarying glances, accepting no differences, acknowledging no differentiations. Verily from his eyes does nectar flow!

Islam too holds mercy and compassion in high esteem. Prophet Mohammed was asked what charity was and he replied: "It is to give a sip of water to the thirsty, to guide the stranger who has lost his way, and to extend the hand of friendship to one you know and to one you know not."

Of equal import is the declaration in the Old Testament: "If I speak in the tongues of men and of angels but have not love, I am like tinkling cymbals and sounding brass" (I Corinthians).

There is the tradition of non-covetousness too — 'keeping up with the Joneses' was never India's tradition. There is a negative as well as a positive connotation to this: first, do not covet what another has; second, be ever ready to give up yours for the sake of another. An example of the first is Bharata (the younger brother of Rama, in the epic *Ramayana*) who neither coveted nor accepted the kingdom of Ayodhya which his scheming mother Kaikeyi had plotted to secure for him — it was his for the asking!

The second is the epic tale of Prince Devavrata, of the *Mahabharata* fame, who took the vow of celibacy just so that his love-smitten father, Emperor Santanu could marry his beloved Matsyagandhi, without the latter fearing that the kingdom would pass to Devavrata's offspring and not to hers. Because of such total renunciation, he was called Bhishma or the one who proclaimed a terrible vow and, more importantly, fulfilled it without reneging! What a far cry these two tradition-setters' lives to the present-day trend of *kissa kursi ka* — the tale is that of the chair, the story is of power and pelf.

Then there is the tradition of absolute and unswerving adherence to Truth — exemplified in the lives of Harishchandra and Rama as reflected in the nation's motto: *Satyameva jayate*.

We have not looked at traditions here in the sense of festivals and celebrations, observances and beliefs. The few traditions highlighted here among many others are not empty enunciations of the impossible or declarations of the unattainable. Instead, we have to appreciate that it is because they stem from eternal verities, they help men and women to blossom forth in their own lives into the fullness of achievement, awakened to the tradition of the fragrance of lives well and truly lived.

9 | Parallels in Other Religions

Although passing references to beliefs and practices are there in other religions, too, the rituals and traditions that we have seen thus far are principally of Hinduism. The former too have what anthropologists call 'rites of passage'. Apart from similarly marking out the main stages in one's life — from birth through adulthood into marriage, husbandry and death, these provide a bridge to the past as well as keep social bonding and continuity of tradition alive.

Birth, post-natal rites of cleansing, naming — different religions celebrate these differently, the core being synchronous, however. To mark the entry of the baby into the Christian community, some water from the font in the church is poured on its

head, following the reading of a text from the Gospel, with the priest announcing, "I baptise you, in the name of the Father, the Son and the Holy Spirit" (suggestive of the *Teenmurti* of Hinduism). When the child, if a Catholic, is about seven and has imbibed appropriate religious instruction, he receives the First Communion, followed by Confirmation.

In Judaism the (male) child is circumcised on the eighth day after birth, as a sign of the renewal of the pact between God and His people. The name is conferred then through a public declaration among friends and family. The child (again, male) is accepted into the community around the age of thirteen, at a ceremony called Bar Mitzvah, Son of the Commandment. This is when he wears the *talleth,* cloak and the *tefillin,* an amulet or small leather

ABOVE
Catholic children at their First Communion, cleansing their hands with holy water

pouch (strapped to the arm or forehead, enclosing strips of parchment inscribed with Hebrew scripture), and reads sections of the *Torah* prescribed for the day. For girls, there was no corresponding ceremony. But in progressive Judaism, there is now a Bar Mitzvah for them too.

There is no 'initiation' of a child into Islam; a child born of a Muslim father is automatically a Muslim. The only other way of becoming a Muslim is by conversion, where a non-Muslim has to go through *shahadat* testifying to his subscribing fully to the tenets of Islam. He has to feel and declare: *Ash-hadu Allah ilaaha il-lal-laahu wa ash hadu an na muhammadan abdu-hoo wa rasooluh,* I declare that none is worthy of worship except Allah and I declare that Muhammad is His servant and His messenger. With this he becomes a Muslim and his intention being pure, he is forgiven all past sins.

There is no particular ceremony in Islam at birth or soon thereafter; even circumcision is not obligatory, although it has become customary almost universally. Boys are usually named after a famous person or Prophet (like Musa or Suleiman) or glorifying an Islamic cultural ideal — Ali (noble,

ABOVE
Syedna Mohammed Burhanuddin, the spiritual head of Dawoodi Bohra Muslims, with his followers, officiating at a nikah

exalted), Abdul Raheem (servant of the Most Merciful Allah), or Omar (of long life). Similarly, girls could be named Fatima (after the Prophet's daughter), Jamila (beautiful), Ayesha (after the Prophet's wife) or Monira (the Enlightened).

The Jains observe a 10-day period of cleansing after birth, ending with the *priyodbhava samskar*. At *namakaran* on the eleventh, thirteenth or twenty-ninth day after birth, the child is given its name. For the boys the name is usually from one of the 1,008 names of the *jinasahasranaam*, while the girls are generally named after famous ladies of legends and *Puranas*.

The Sikhs do not have any prescribed ritual at birth; in some families, five verses of *Japji Sahib* are recited into the child's ears. The following *shabads* are popular: *Satguru sachai ditta bhej…Parmesar ditta banna…,* the guru has sent the child; the child born by destiny will live long. And God is the bulwark. It is interesting to note that Sikhism holds up from birth the equality of the sexes. The *Guru Granth Sahib* acclaims: Akal Purakh has blessed the birth of the child. To rejoice at the birth of a son but feel sad or inferior at the birth of a girl is against the principles of the Sikh faith. The child is named (followed by 'Singh' for boys and 'Kaur' for girls), usually after the gurus or signifying an ideal or an exalted concept – for boys, Arjun (after the guru), Amandeep (light of peace), or Harjot (Divine Spirit); followed by the suffix Singh; and for girls, Harleen (utterly lost in Hari or Vishnu), Updesh (she of sage counsel), or Gagandeep (light of the skies), followed by the suffix Kaur.

Around the age of 11 to 16, *dastar bandi,* the ceremonial tying of the Sikh turban, for the first time, takes place in a *gurdwara*. The five K's are crucial to the Sikh faith — *kesh*, hair (unshorn from birth), *kanga*, comb, *kachcha*, drawers, *karha*, steel bracelet, and *kirpan*, sword in its sheath. Each has a unique significance and symbolism. *Kesh* is God's gift and should not be lightly discarded; a man should bow his head only before a guru and not to the barber; and uncut hair is a sign of humility and conscious lack of pride in one's appearance. *Kanga* signifies the need to keep hair clean, it being God's endowment. *Kachcha*, the symbol of self-control was, in earlier times, very suitable, convenient and appropriate for warriors. *Karha* signifies that God has neither beginning nor end; a symbol of enduring bond to the community, the Khalsa, *kari* meaning 'link'. And *kirpan* is a testament to the martial background and history, and a reminder of the obligation to fight against injustice and to defend the weak and the good.

The most important ceremony of initiation among the Sikhs is the *Amrit Samskara* — the equivalent, so to speak, of baptism — when the child is initiated into the Khalsa as an *amritdhari*. After the ritual bath and putting on clean clothes (with the 5 K's in position), the candidate — boy or girl — being deemed fit to be accepted, appears before five select Sikhs, who must be *amritdharis* themselves. One of them reads out at a verse chosen at random from the *Granth Sahib*. Then the candidate asks for permission from the congregation for admission to the Khalsa, which is generally granted to the fervent shout of *Bole so nihal sat sree akal*, whosoever speaketh would be blessed, God is truth and everlasting. Then the *amrit*, ambrosia, which is sugar dissolved in water in an iron bowl and stirred with a *kirpan* by the Khalsa (of the aforesaid five Sikhs), accompanied by the recitation of the *Japji Sahib* (Guru Nanak), *Jap Sahib, Sudha Swayas* and *Benti Chaupai* (Guru Gobind Singh) and *Anand Sahib* (Guru Amardas). Then the *amrit* is spooned out to the aspirant and is sprinkled on the eyes and head, what is left of the *amrit* in the bowl being drunk by the candidate.

With recognition comes obligation; and so the *amritdharis* have stringent do's and don'ts. They must believe in the teachings of the 10 gurus and the *Granth Sahib;* recite a daily five *banis,* collection of hymns; meticulously don the five K's; live on honest earnings of their own; treat all human beings as absolutely equal; and spread the name of God. They must not have any truck with those who have no belief in God; nor have recourse to intoxicants of any kind; nor believe in magic and rituals. Very severe stipulations indeed! Hence the *amrit samskara* is not to be, and infact, is not lightly undertaken!

In Zoroastrianism, the mother and child are kept sequestered at home, from the imperative of avoiding infection to them. At the *Para Haoma* ceremony, the baby has his first drink — a sip of consecrated *homa* juice, to pray for and augur good health. *Navjote* signifies the formal admission of the child (boy or girl) into the faith between seven and eleven years of age. After *nahaan,* a special bath, the child stands on a small dais and the mother performs the *Achoo Michoo* ceremony in which she rotates some select objects around his head, invoking the blessings of the seven *Amesha Spentas* on the young candidate. After special prayers, the *kushti,* made up of 72 fine woollen strands, is tied three times round the waist with the short ends hanging about the waist. It is worn over a shirt called *sadreh,* unlike the Hindu *yajnopavita* which is always worn on the bare body.

Among the excerpts of special prayers which the young one has to recite is the refrain of *Ashem Vohu: Ashem vohu vahishtam asti ushta asti, ushta ahmai hyat ashai vahishtai ashem,* righteousness is the best good. It is radiant happiness. Radiant happiness comes to one who is righteous for the sake of righteousness alone. Navjote concludes with the recitation of the *Doa Tandorosti* prayer for the child's wellbeing.

Now to marriage: traditionally, a Jewish marriage is only between two Jews, as is the case with the Zoroastrians, too. If a non-Jew wishes to marry a Jew, he or she must convert to Judaism. However, reformed Jews make a departure, so long as there is the promise to bring up the offspring in the Jewish faith. The ceremony itself is very simple: the groom puts a ring on

LEFT
A festive mood, at a Jewish wedding

the bride's finger at the *kiddushin* ceremony, followed by the *ketubbah*, setting out the marriage contract setting forth the specific indemnity by the husband in the event of a divorce. *Nissum*, nuptials, follow, before seven witnesses and 10 adult males, and it is the final public avowal of the marriage. There is much merrymaking thereafter, during which the groom drinks up the wine and smashes the glass under his feet, symbolic of the destruction of the Temple of Jerusalem.

ABOVE
A priest administering the vows to a Christian couple at their wedding

The Christian marriage is a sacrament — an exercise of profound religious (and moral) significance, denoting the direct intervention of God in communicating His grace to those who wish to unite themselves in matrimony. In Catholicism, this union is inviolable and unbreakable. In all sections of the Christian religion, as a whole, however, the virtues of loving cohabitation, mutual assistance and affection, along with faithfulness — in prosperous times and at others, in joy and in sorrow are paramount. The wedding ceremony is usually in a church, before an assembly of friends and relatives and is conducted by the priest, with select readings from the Bible, to the accompaniment of appropriate hymns. Following a brief question and answer interlude, when both the groom and the bride declare their intention publicly 'to have and to hold, in sickness and in health, for richer or for poorer', and their promise to love each other, the priest pronounces them to be man and wife. The cornerstone of the nuptial edifice is the element of 'reciprocal' commitment.

The process of assimilation in India is evident from the fact that, in Kerala Christian weddings, the *tali* (the Tamil/Kerala equivalent of the *mangalasutra*) plays an important role. Among the Syrian Christians, it is customary for the groom to give a new sari to the bride, called *mantra kodi*, from the threads of which his sister makes a chord of several strands to which is added the *tali* in the shape of a leaf pendant bearing the sign of the Cross. This is tied round the bride's neck, as indeed in the Hindu ceremony.

Although wedding is regarded as a secular affair in Buddhism, it has come to be performed ceremonially, to the accompaniment of recitations from the *vandana*, homage, *tisarana*, triple refuge, and *panchshila*, the Five Precepts. Then the groom recites this from the *Digha Nayika*: And this towards my wife I undertake, to love and respect her, be kind and considerate, faithful and delegate management of the home and provide gifts to please her. The wife, in turn, recites another verse, signifying her faithfulness, dedication to careful and efficient management of the home and to hospitality to the in-laws and friends, alongside of her commitment to the discharge of her wifely responsibilities with love and efficiency. Here again, there is a 'give and take' between the couple! The ceremony ends with the recitation of the *Mangala Sutta*.

The Jain wedding is more elaborate, with as many as nine rituals, the principal of which are: *lagana lekhan*, delineation of the *muhurtam* and *patrika vaachan*, the ceremonial and public reading of the invitation followed by *sagai*, formal engagement. Then follows *phere* when, seated beside each other, the couple take the seven vows. At *kanyavaran* thereafter, the bride's parents present her to the groom, with the father avowing before the assemblage that he has done so. Then the couple goes four times round the *havan*, sacrificial fire, with one end of the bride's sari tied to the groom's shawl, to the accompanying recitation of hymns. This concludes the ceremony.

The Islamic ceremony is the simplest. Wedding in Islam is not a sacrament; it is a contract, pure and simple. After the *mehr*, dowry, is negotiated and fixed, the *nikah* ceremony takes place, when the bride is asked, in the presence of two witnesses, if she accepts the groom and the *mehr* and on her saying '*qabool hai*', the ceremony is over. The *nikahnama*, marriage contract, incorporating the rights of the bride, is concluded. The element of consent, here again, affirmed before witnesses, the right to *mehr* as a redoubtable insurance of protection to the bride and the obligation of the man to offer maintenance to the divorced wife, are worthy of note.

In Zoroastrianism, at the Parsi wedding in India, the bride's mother welcomes the groom with a *sindhura tilak*, vermillion mark, as the *baraat* arrives. The priest throws rice over the couple and coconut water is poured at the groom's feet, while a person with a glowing flame is in attendance. Seated on either side of a curtain, the couple's consent is verified by the priest who ties a long piece of cloth around, enclosing them. The couple holds each other's right hand, as the *Yatha Ahuvairyo* is read. Then the curtain between them is dropped and the couple, united in matrimony, rise to the acclamation of those present.

Anand Karaj, the Sikh wedding ceremony literally translates into the 'ceremony of bliss'. There are the age-old social customs like the *surma pawai*, application of *kohl*, collyrium, to the groom's eyes, usually by his *bhabhi*, the groom's sister-in-law. At the *milni*, the first encounter between the couple at the ceremony, *shabads* are sung and the families greet each other. The couple is seated before the *Granth Sahib* and the priest or the elder who is conducting the ceremony, explains the obligations of marriage to them; appropriate hymns from the *Granth Sahib* are read. This is followed by the *laawaan* when, holding the two ends of a scarf, the groom leads the bride four times around the holy book. This solemnises the marriage, whereafter the *doli* leaves for the bride's new home. As she leaves the parental home or the venue of the wedding, she throws wheat grains over her shoulder,

RIGHT
A solemn scene of dedication and commitment at Anand Karaj, *the Sikh wedding*

signifying that she is paying off her debts to her parents for their affection and care through the years.

We may look now at the final journey of man, be he Christian, Jew or Muslim, Buddhist, Jain or Sikh. The first three religions consider that upon death, the deceased is reunited with God. The latter three, as also the Hindu, reckon it as the prelude to the commencement of a new chapter in *samsara chakra,* cycle of births and deaths. The ways of dealing with the body bereft of life are basically two: burial or cremation, except for the Zoroastrians who consign the body to the Tower of Silence — even in death the body could and should be of use to birds of prey that also need to survive; besides, this avoids pollution of the atmosphere and the elements. As death is seen to approach, the head priests are summoned to recite the *pater*, prayer for repentance, and a few drops of the *haoma* or pomegranate juice are fed to the dying person's lips. We have seen *Gangajal* being similarly administered to the dying Hindu.

RIGHT
His Holiness the Dalai Lama leading the monks at prayer

The Buddhists cremate their dead, at a solemn ceremony with monks preceding the coffin chanting prayers; the ash is preserved in an urn. The Jews practice burial. One of the children intones the *Kaddish,* an ancient prayer which is recited during the period of mourning, as also at the anniversaries. *Keriah,* a symbolic small tear in the mourners' clothes, indicates a grieving heart. During the seven-day mourning, close relatives abstain from work, with men not shaving or cutting their hair for 30 days. Following the eulogy by the Rabbi or a close friend, the coffin is interred.

The Jains too cremate their dead, at the earliest possible, so as to avoid the possibility of pollution to any living being. Even the cremation ground should be bereft of grass or insects so as not to harm even plant and insect life — a rededication, as it were, to the Jain creed of non-violence, in death as in life. Cremation follows a pattern, with the eldest son sprinkling water over the body (brought in a bier, wrapped in cloth), going round three times and lighting the pyre, to the chanting of the *namokar mantra.* The remains are collected in bags and buried, as immersion in a river will pollute the waters; earth assimilates them easily, with no harm to anyone. As in Sikhism, the Jains also desist from loud wailing, grieving and the observance of anniversaries, as they believe that the dead are reborn instantly.

Christians bury their dead. After a particular liturgy and prayers by the priest, the coffin containing the body is buried, with close relatives and friends throwing in handfuls of earth in a symbolic act of irreversible — Dust thou art, and to dust thou returneth. The departed being is deemed to be consigned to the hands of God and to eternal bliss, avoiding condemnation or punishment of any sort.

As in all other religions, in Islam, too, after *gosal,* the cleansing bath, and dressing of the body, it is wrapped in a *kafan,* a white winding sheet, and taken in *janaaza,* a burial procession, on the shoulders of relatives and friends, with burial prayers — *dua* or *fatiha* for the dead — being recited all the way as the cortege proceeds to final resting place. The body is buried, resting on its right side, with the face turned towards *kaaba*, to betoken the undying faith of the deceased. A large stone is placed on the body before earth is thrown in to close the grave. Islam does not countenance wailing or demonstrations of excessive grief, for, has it not been said: *Lilaha va inna illaha raziun,* we have come from God and unto Him we return. What is there, then, to grieve?

The Sikhs regard death as a natural process and an indication of Divine will. Hence there is neither the need to grieve nor the call for annual *sraaddha* ceremonies. During the 10-day mourning period, the *Granth Sahib* is read in the house of the deceased, the hymns focus on acceptance of the Divine will and espousal of the attitude of detachment. Bathed and dressed along with the five K's, the body is cremated as holy hymns are chanted, with the eldest son lighting the funeral pyre. On the third day after cremation, the bones are collected, washed in milk and consigned to a holy river.

The foregoing is just a bird's eye-view of the striking parallels in the rites of passage in the leading religions of the world. But it establishes that, in vital areas of life and living, there is a remarkable identity of perceptions in all religions as to the oneness of the ultimate Truth. The revolutionary Tamil poet Subramanya Bharati puts this across splendidly:

> *Fire-worshipping Brahmins, Muslims who*
> *daily to the Quarters pray, and Christians*
> *who bow before the Cross in churches —*
> *All worship but one God, the Being*
> *abiding in every being. One God*
> *alone in all the world there is.*
> *Let us have no quarrels about it.*

10 | Prayer

'Communication', and that too 'instant communication' is the buzzword of our globalised market economy. If inter-personal, inter-institutional and inter-governmental communication are the essence of our lives today, how much more important it is to have one's lines open with the Creator of all, the Supreme or whatever each religion may choose to call It! Most reassuringly, too, this is one thing on which there is no disagreement between religions — there is consensus that 'more things are wrought by prayer....'

While the pith and substance are same, of course, techniques and practices vary. The Hindu does a *puja* as a ritual enjoined for special occasions and days, although

traditional, orthodox practitioners do undertake daily *pujas*, to their *ishta devata*, deity of their choice, like Shiva in the shape of a *salagrama*, granite-like stones, or idols of Rama/Krishna and the like. *Shodasopachaaram* are the 16 principal steps of *puja*. They are: *dhyaanam*, where one contemplates the deity as a prelude to the *puja, aavaahanam*, invoking the deity, *aasanam*, offering a seat, *paadyam*, water for cleansing of the feet, *arghyam*, water for cleansing the palms, *aachamanam*, as during *sandhyavandana*, *snaanam*, ablutions, in the form of *abishekam*, i.e. bathing the deity with pure water and various other liquids and substances, *vastram*, dressing the deity, *gandham*, applying sandal paste, *pushpam*, floral offerings, included during the *archanam*, calling out the 108/1008 names (*ashtottara/sahastranama*) of the deity with flowers, *akshata* and *kumkumam*, as the case may be, *dhoopam*, incense, *deepam*, a small lamp with a cotton wick usually soaked in *ghee*, *naivedyam*, offering of food, sweets and fruits, *neeraajanam*, offering the camphor flame, and *pradakshina namaskaaram*, circumambulation of and prostration before the deity.

There are rigid prescriptions and prohibitions about each of these steps. To mention just a few: only whole flowers with fragrance, and not petals should be used. Flowers should preferably be those that have

blossomed that day — the lotus being the exception, as also *tulsi* and *bilva*. Vishnu should not be worshipped with *akshata*, Shiva with *kevda*, screwpine (*Pandanus odoratissimus*), Devi with fine grass, and Ganesha with *tulsi*. Incidentally, fine grass (*arugampul*, in Tamil), taboo for Devi, is the favourite of Ganesha! Red flowers are the best for Devi, as are *tulsi* for Vishnu, and *bilva* and the flowers of the *dhatura* for Shiva.

Similarly, the substances that are included as being appropriate for *abishekam* are: turmeric water, cow's milk (raw, not boiled), yoghurt, honey, *panchamrutam* (a mixture of fruits with honey, sugar candy, raisins and *gur*, unrefined sugar), tender coconut water, cane juice, juice of a lemon, pomegranate or citrus, liquid sandal, rosewater, saffron-scented water, freshly cooked rice and in the case of Shiva, Ganesha and Kartikeya, and *vibhuti*, sacred ash. Each one of these is indicative of its potential to confer certain benefits, e.g. milk for longevity, yoghurt for fecundity, pomegranate juice for decimation of enemies, *panchamrutam* for *mukti*, liberation, *chandan*, sandal, for regal qualities and wealth, rice for agricultural prosperity and lemon for banishment of the fear of death.

Most important is total concentration (and symbiosis of the body, speech and mind) during *puja*, on the part of the *karta* or the doer thereof; unnecessary disturbances and needless speech are to be totally avoided. This is only to remind that all worship and all prayers are to be *bhakti*-based. *Bhakti* is total immersion of the self in that Higher Self, whatever be its name.

In the Hindu lore, *bhakti* is of nine genres — *navavidha bhakti*. Focusing on an *ishta devata*, God of choice (for each individual), these are: *shravanam*, hearing the names of the Lord or His *gunas* and exploits, *smaranam*, ruminating constantly on them, *kirtanam*, singing the Lord's names or extolling His greatness, *archanam*, *paada sevanam*, worshipping at His feet, *daasyam*, undertaking the task of service unto Him, *sakhyam*, envisioning and treating Him as a *sakha*, friend and *aatma nivedanam*, unqualified surrender of the self.

PAGE 96
A devout Hindu offering water from a holy teertha *in* abhisheka, *ablution of a deity, to a Shivalinga; with the Nandi bull gazing in rapture*

PAGE 97
The tulsi *(basil) plant, worshipped in almost every Hindu home*

Now to prayer in Christianity: the basic or the morning prayer is the Lord's prayer. It is one of obeisance and respect — 'Our Father who art in Heaven, hallowed be Thy name', a plea for the day's pabulum — 'Give us today our daily bread', a supplication for forgiveness — 'Forgive us our sins, as we forgive those who sin against us', ending with an earnest prayer — 'Do not bring us to the test, but deliver us from all evil'. The foregoing encompass the basic tenets of Christianity, namely, that God is the provider of all, that His will is supreme, and that forgiveness and charity are to be practiced ceaselessly.

The evening prayer is the rosary, offered (among the Catholics) to St. Mary. And at bedtime, again, the Lord's prayer is recited, along with an

LEFT
A Catholic priest breaking the bread before the congregation, signifying the body of Christ

offering of thanks for all His bounty that day and pleading for the strength and the will to face the morrow with equal strength and determination. There are, of course, special prayers, as during Easter and Lent — the latter calls for fasting, too.

Sunday, the Day of the Sabbath, is considered to be the Lord's Day (to mark the Resurrection). Christians observe it as a day of special prayers, going to church unfailingly, almost always as a family. The Catholics celebrate Mass on Sundays, the first part consisting of select readings from the Bible, followed by a sermon. The second part is the Eucharist — recalling a key moment in the Last Supper of Christ with his disciples, when he gave them bread to eat and wine to drink, representing his body and his blood. A symbolic distribution of bread and wine is made to the congregation at the end — in moments of intense devotion and faithful recall, rather like the *amrit* of Sikhism.

The Sikh religion, too, calls for prayer, morning, evening and night. It is like the *trikaala sandhyavandana*, although there are no procedures and rituals; wholehearted recitation of portions of the *Granth Sahib* and other segments of the *Japji Sahib*, *Jaap Sahib* and *Savaiye* is what is prescribed. The morning prayer consists of the three latter, starting with the celebrated opening verse of *Ik Onkar: Ik Onkar, satnam, karta purakh, nirbhav, nirvair, akaal murat, ajuni, sehbang,* 'Oh Thou, the one and only Onkara! Truth is thy name; thou art the doer of all; thou art fearless, without enemies; thou art the Eternal Being; devoid of the bondage of the cycle of birth and death; and *sui generis*'.

The evening prayer, *Rehras Sahib*: is for peace. *Dukh daru sukh rog bhaya, ja sukh taam na hoi, tu karta karna main nahin, ja hau kari na hoi,* sorrow is the medicament, happiness is the disease, for in happiness one does not think of Thee. Thou art the Doer, not me; whatever I do just does not happen. In other words, once again, the Lord is All; no one else matters.

The bed-time prayer *Kirtan Sohila: Jaiye ghar kirat aakhiye, karte ka hoi bicharo, tit ghar gaao Sohila, sivaro sirjan haro, tum gaao mere nirbhav ka Sohila*

ABOVE
A Hindu pandit in meditation, on the banks of the Ganga at Kedarghat, Kashi

enunciates: In that household where the *kirat* (*kirti*), the fame of Bhagwan abounds, where the thoughts are focused on it, sing the Sohila there; remember The Name, and sing the Sohila in honour of my Fearless (Being). The story goes that a Banjara Sikh beseeched Guru Arjun Dev to teach him some shabads so that he might be rid of fear at night from bandits, robbers and supernatural beings. The Guru put together three verses from Guru Nanakdev's time that Guru Angad Singh had prescribed for being sung at night and one verse each of Guru Ramdas and himself and passed on all five *shabads* to him as Sohila, to be sung in the *Raag Gowri* at bedtime, as a guarantor of protection; this is what is in vogue since then.

Among the five pillars of the Islamic faith is *salaat*, prayer, the others being *imaan*, faith, *saum*, fasting, *zakat*, charity and *Haj*, pilgrimage to the Holy Shrine. Prayer is to Allah alone, for He is One, the most powerful, and He alone is worthy of worship, none other being so worthy. He is the Creator; He was not created by anyone. He is pure and blemishless.

Prayer is obligatory for every Muslim on attaining puberty and being of sound mind; such *fard*, obligatory prayer, has to be said five times a day. *Sunna* prayers are supererogatory; and mainly accompany the daily five and the two Id prayers — like the noon congregational prayers on *Jumma*, Fridays and *Tawaf*, the Haj prayer. And finally, *Nafi*, optional prayer, which is purely voluntary. The Prophet held these up to his disciples "as an example of the five rivers by which Allah washes away sins."

The five daily prayers are *salat al-fajr* (at dawn); *salat al-zuhr* (at noon), *salat al-'asr* (in the afternoon), *salat al-maghrib* (in the evening); and *salat al-'isha* (at night). A specific number of *rak'ahs* is prescribed for each, ranging from two to four. The hour of prayer is announced or *azaan* publicly by the muezzin. The procedure is set: standing, the supplicant states his intention, raises his hands and intones, *Bismillah-e-Rehman-e-Rahim*: Allah is the most great!; then he recites the first *surah* of the *Quran* (*al-Fatiha*); he bends forwards till his palms touch his knees; then he prostrates, with his knees; then his hands and

forehead to touch the ground; he kneels again; and prostrates a second time likewise — this is one *rak'ah*.

The type of clothes to be worn by a Muslim at prayer is also laid down. Gold and silk is taboo. *Wuzu,* ritual cleansing, has to be undertaken before praying — of hands upto the wrists, arms upto the elbows, mouth, nose, neck and face, and feet upto the ankles. Seated in a clean place, and declaring his *niyat,* intention to pray, the Muslim adopts the *qibla* which, simply, is the direction of Mecca — all Muslims all over the world must face the *kaabaa* there. The *niyat* is all-important, for it signifies that he prays out of pure love and adoration of Allah and not for any other external or material reason or desire.

Other religions, too, have their own prayers and systems of praying. The core, however, is that through prayer, and calling out the Lord's name,

ABOVE
A throng of devotees around the sarovar *(holy tank) at the Sikh shrine Harmandir Sahib, Golden Temple, Amritsar*

one establishes an intense and immediate connection with the Almighty, without the need for intermediaries.

Thus, as, for instance, in the Hindu tradition too, the *nama japa,* recitation of the Lord's name is enough, if only it comes from a heart soaked in *bhakti*; or the tears and sobs that pour forth from a Muslim as he listens to the moving tale of the massacre at Karbala; or the sorrow that wells up in a Christian as he hears the story of the Son of God being nailed to the Cross.

'More things are wrought by prayer than this world dreams of' — wrought equally for the Hindu, the Muslim, the Christian, the Jew, the Buddhist, the Jain and the Sikh! In this again, they are all one.

And so it is that we come to the end of these brief glimpses of rituals and traditions. We have seen that many rituals have withered away, under the onslaught of rationalism, or through ignorance of their rationale; many traditions have been forgotten or abandoned. But it would be good if the questioning mind acts even now, to revive, to streamline or at the end of it all, even to abandon some or all of them, heeding the exhortation of the *rasika*, connoisseur, in Kalidasa's *Malavikagnimitra*:

> *Puraanamityeva na saadhu sarvam*
> *na chapi kaavyam navamityavadyam.*

Accept nothing as good merely because it is old. Reject nothing as bad merely because it is new!